Your Towns and Cities in the Great

Glasgow
in the Great War

Your Towns and Cities in the Great War

Glasgow
in the Great War

Derek Tait

Pen & Sword
MILITARY

First published in Great Britain in 2016 by
PEN & SWORD MILITARY
an imprint of
Pen and Sword Books Ltd
47 Church Street
Barnsley
South Yorkshire S70 2AS

ISBN 978 1 47382 808 7

Printed and bound in England
by CPI Group (UK) Ltd, Croydon, CR0 4YY

Typeset in Times New Roman

Pen & Sword Books Ltd incorporates the imprints of
Pen & Sword Archaeology, Atlas, Aviation, Battleground, Discovery,
Family History, History, Maritime, Military, Naval, Politics, Railways,
Select, Social History, Transport, True Crime, and Claymore Press,
Frontline Books, Leo Cooper, Praetorian Press, Remember When,
Seaforth Publishing and Wharncliffe.

For a complete list of Pen and Sword titles please contact
Pen and Sword Books Limited
47 Church Street, Barnsley, South Yorkshire, S70 2AS, England

E-mail: enquiries@pen-and-sword.co.uk
Website: **www.pen-and-sword.co.uk**

Contents

Chapter One

1914: Eager for a Fight

Rising tensions in Europe and the assassination of Franz Ferdinand in Sarajevo, led to Austria-Hungary's declaration of war on Serbia. This led to the Central Powers, which included Germany and Austria-Hungary, and the Allies, which included the British Empire, the French Republic and the Russian Empire, to declare war on each other which led to the commencement of the First World War on 28 July 1914.

On Monday 3 August, *The Dundee Evening Telegraph* reported a story under the headline A SCOTSMAN AT GLASGOW OFFERS HIMSELF FOR SERVICE IN FRANCE. The story read:

'Animated scenes were witnessed at Glasgow Consular offices today.

At the French Consular office, reservists have already numerously responded to the call and this morning the staff were busy arranging for their transit to France.

A Scotsman called and offered himself for service for France. The Consul informed him that he had not received instructions to accept volunteers. The man seemed a likely fellow, and well set up, and would doubtless find some other way of getting to France.

Russian Reservists, mostly miners in the Lanarkshire Coalfields, have called and intimated their names and addresses, so that when the Russian army requires them, they will be ready to go.

Some anxiety is felt in Glasgow regarding tourists now on the continent.

A gentleman called today at Adams Express Companionship Office and related his experiences. He arrived back today after being on holiday in Germany. He stated that he met passengers on the Hook of Holland steamer, who had been cavalierly turned out of their train when approaching the German frontier, and had

Archduke Franz Ferdinand of Austria. Ferdinand's assassination in Sarajevo on 28 June 1914 led to Austria-Hungary's declaration of war on Serbia which ultimately led to the beginning of the First World War.

to sit by the side of the railway for hours while a Dutch train was being brought for them. Many carried their baggage for miles and crossed the frontier on foot.'

Panic buying of foodstuff was noted in *The Daily Record* just before the announcement of war:

'Glasgow shopkeepers were again inundated with orders yesterday. The scenes of Saturday were repeated but the panic of buying was more general. Despite the Shops Act, the meal-hours of the shop assistants were curtailed in order that customers might have attention and the crush at the counters be relieved.

Unlike Saturday, when the wealthier people were laying in stocks, the demand for provisions yesterday was more general in the poorer districts. The wives of artisans were more in evidence and were buying as much meal, flour, bacon and sugar as their means could afford.

As a rule, they carried their purchases away with them. But there were larger orders which had to be delivered by messenger and van, and as these were occupied with dealing with goods purchased on Saturday, deliveries could not be guaranteed.

A stop had also to be put to letter orders, which form a large proportion of the business of the more extensive firms. The cash orders on hand were sufficient to keep the assistants fully employed for some days and shopkeepers could afford to ignore anything which was not a cash transaction. The heavy demand for supplies soon exhausted stocks. Late in the afternoon, a large number of shopkeepers were completely sold out of foodstuffs. In the afternoon, the state of exhaustion was almost general and many shops suspended business altogether. It was not a rare experience for one customer to buy goods at a price, while the customer immediately behind had to pay an advanced figure. For instance, sugar in the morning could be bought at 2½d but in the afternoon, the price had gone up to 4½d. As announced in *The Daily Record and Sunday Mail* yesterday, prices were raised all round, and householders found the cost of food entailing an extra expense of from 15 to 20 per cent more. Unless war on the part of Great Britain is definitely averted for the present, a further rise in the price of foodstuffs is most probable this week'.

Meanwhile, crowds of 20,000 gathered in heavy rain at St James Watt Street to watch naval men call into the Mercantile Marine Office to collect their papers and travelling tickets. The crowd quickly grew in number and by 8 o'clock there were 3,000-4,000 people gathered. Mounted police were posted alongside the office because of disorder caused on the previous night.

The reservists arrived singly and after they had received their books and tickets, they returned home before preparing for the journey to Portsmouth at 9 o'clock. Many were accompanied by their wives and children, some of whom were crying. The men were cheered and clapped as they walked through the crowds. *The Daily Record* reported:

'Central Station was, as on the previous night, besieged by an immense crowd of people, whose enthusiasm exceeded their sense of decorum. At a moderate estimate, there were 20,000 men, women and children clamouring for admittance to the departure platform.

A force of 300 policemen, assisted by the mounted constabulary, who had been withdrawn from the Mercantile Marine Offices, attempted to keep order under the direction of Chief Constable Stevenson and his assistant, Chief Constable Orr. The policemen generally acted with tact and took the crowd in hand good humouredly, pitting their mobile strength against the crush of the crowd to keep a passage clear.

The scene was reminiscent of those which accompanied the departure of the troops for the South African War. Even the reservists had to fight their way to the train by means of a vigorous use of their elbows.

The special train at No.1 platform, where Mr Killen, Assistant Superintendent of the Line, and Stationmaster Allison were looking after the arrangements, was bordered by a long line of relatives of the departing naval men.

There were affecting partings, but on the whole everyone was cheerful and as the train steamed out, such a cheer arose from a crowd who had gained access to No.3 platform as drowned the sound of the train whistle itself. The reservists, leaning out of the carriage windows, waved their caps vigorously and returned the cheering with goodwill.

A number of men who were ordered to Chatham and one or two who missed the Portsmouth special proceeded to London by the train at 10.45. Though the vast majority of the crowd had left the station, there were enough spectators remaining to give the second contingent of reservists a hearty send-off.'

On 4 August, newspapers posted announcements in their windows stating that Britain had declared war on Germany.

People of foreign descent were quickly rounded up and detained. Anyone with a German sounding accent soon came under suspicion of being a spy.

The railways were taken under government control under the Regulations of Forces Act of 1871. Local businesses were asked to supply motor vehicles for use by the army and businesses in and around Glasgow were asked to supply horses.

A notice appeared in *The Daily Record* of 5 August stating:

'Special orders were issued last night empowering commanding officers to requisition horses and carriages, vessels and aircraft, and conferring authority on the officers to issue warrants on householders in any military districts for the billeting of troops.'

Horses fared badly at the front. Many were killed by artillery fire and were affected by skin conditions and poison gas. Hundreds of thousands of horses died during the conflict, many of them requisitioned from British civilians. However, Lord Kitchener stated that no horse under 15 hands should be confiscated. This was because many children showed a concern about the welfare of their ponies.

Young men rushed to join the army. The 1/5th (City of Glasgow)

The Glasgow Highlanders ready for home defence. The Highlanders gave a hearty response to the mobilisation order. A group of territorials wait for orders at their headquarters in Greendyke Street.

Horses being used to transport equipment for a Glasgow battalion of the territorials. Many horses were requisitioned from private owners, farms and businesses. Most suffered a terrible fate although the RSPCA and the Royal Army Veterinary Corps did their best to treat and look after wounded horses.

Battalion was formed in August at Garnethill as part of the Highland Light Infantry Brigade. Other regiments formed in August included the 1/6th (City of Glasgow) Battalion (formed at Yorkshill Street), the 1/7th (Blythswood) Battalion (formed at Bridgeton) and the 1/9th (Glasgow Highland) Battalion formed at Greendyke Street).

The Daily Record of Sunday 16 August reported on the swearing-in ceremony of the Civic Guard movement. The article stated:

'Glasgow's civic guard is already a puissant force. To date almost a thousand men have been enrolled in the city. Fine, stalwart fellows they are for the most part. Numbers of them have seen active service and the majority have had experience of the

Many men rush to enlist, 1914. As war was announced, men of all ages were keen to enlist and showed much patriotism. Many saw it as an adventure, a way to escape unemployment or their humdrum daily lives. Most thought that the war wouldn't last long and would be over by Christmas.

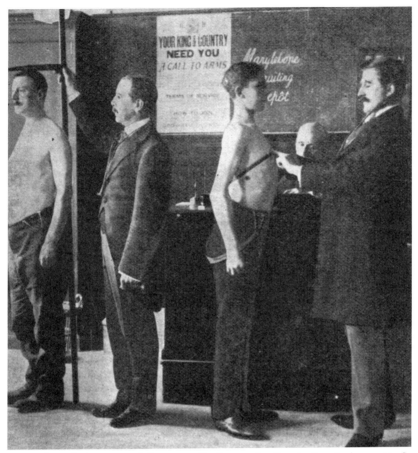

A youth and a man receiving a medical examination before being passed
fit to enlist. In the background is a recruitment poster stating, 'Your
King and country need you'.

Volunteer or Territorial Force.

The swearing-in ceremony took place last night at the police
stations throughout Glasgow. The muster was particularly
gratifying at the Central, the commodious gymnasium in which the
citizen guard assembled for the occasion being well filled.

The names of the special constables having been formally
registered, Bailie James Stewart, the acting officer, administered
the oath, which bound the guard to obey any orders that might be
given them by the Chief Constable or his officers. In answer to the
question of acceptance put by the Bailie, the guard heartily
intimated, "I do".

On behalf of the magistrates, Bailie Stewart then thanked the guard for coming forward and offering their services. It was unfortunate there should be occasion for the formation of such a force but they in Glasgow had no control over the crisis with which the nation was at present faced. He thought it must be very pleasing to the Magistrates, and to the citizens, that so many men had come forward and voluntarily offered their services.'

On 19 August, President Woodrow Wilson announced that America would remain neutral throughout the war.

The first shots by British troops on foreign soil took place on 22 August 1914. A military unit of the 4th Dragoon Guards, comprising 120 men, were sent on a reconnoitring mission ahead of the British Expeditionary Force (BEF). Although members of the BEF had landed a week before, no contact with the enemy had taken place. As forces advanced into France and Belgium, they heard stories from civilians that large numbers of German troops were advancing towards the town of Mons in Belgium. Shortly after, the cavalrymen of the Dragoon Guards encountered the enemy and the first shots taken in Europe since the Battle of Waterloo became the first of millions to be fired over the next four years.

On 26 August, the Battle of Tannenberg began.

On 2 September, the 15th (Service) Battalion (1st Glasgow), more commonly known as the Glasgow Tramways Battalion, was formed by the Lord Provost within the city. Almost 1,000 men left their jobs working on the trams in Glasgow to join the battalion and were paraded in George Square on 7 September. Their manager, James Dalrymple was on hand to address the men who were inspected by the Lord Provost (Sir D.M. Stevenson), accompanied by Colonel Stanley Paterson.

By the end of the week, Glasgow had raised 25,000 men for the regular army. New recruits for the Glasgow Highlanders were drilled on Glasgow Green, smartly dressed in their everyday clothes before uniforms were issued. A company of young men from the Glasgow Steel Roofing Company enlisted together on 7 September.

Amongst other battalions also formed during the early part of September were the Glasgow Boys' Brigade Battalion (16th Service Battalion, 2nd Glasgow). On 10 September, the 17th (Service) Battalion

(3rd Glasgow) was formed by the Chamber of Commerce and briefly moved to Gailes before being sent on to Troon on 13 October. Other battalions formed that month included the 2/5th (City of Glasgow) Battalion, the 2/6th (City of Glasgow) Battalion, the 2/7th (Blythswood) Battalion and the 2/9th (Glasgow Highland) Battalion.

On 5 September, the First Battle of the Marne began. It also marked the commencement of trench warfare as both sides dug in preparing for combat.

The Daily Record carried news of the start of enrolment for Glasgow's Own Battalion on 11 September:

'At St Andrew's Halls, a start was made with the enrolment of ex-members of the Boys' Brigade for Glasgow's Own battalions of Lord Kitchener's Army. One hundred and seventy were attested. The recruiting will continue tomorrow, beginning at three o'clock, and a parade of all those who have been attested will be held in the hall at 7.30 in the evening.

Tomorrow, a start will be made at the Technical College with the enrolment of the Commercial Battalion.

It is expected that the first batch of men will be dispatched on Monday to the training camp at Gailes. The Magistrates' Sub-Committee on recruiting visited the ground in the afternoon to see

Glasgow Highlanders being drilled. Before the first week of September was out, Glasgow had raised 25,000 men for the regular army. The Highlanders are shown, before their uniforms have been issued, receiving instructions at Glasgow Green.

A group of men from the Glasgow Steel Roofing Company who all enlisted together in the early part of September.

A Glasgow recruit lifts his daughter onto his shoulder as she prepares to bid him farewell as he leaves for training.

that everything was in readiness.

Recruiting is proceeding at the headquarters of those Territorial units who have been accepted for foreign service.

Men continue to be sent almost each day to Inverness to join the training for Lochiel's new battalions.'

A story appeared in *The Daily Record* of Saturday 12 September under the headline FIFTY GERMANS ARRESTED IN GLASGOW:

'Instructions have been given by the Secretary of State for Scotland to Glasgow police to arrest every male German under 45 years, who has served in the German army or who has had military experience.

So far about fifty have been arrested and were handed over to the military authorities. They are meanwhile detained at Maryhill Barracks.

It is understood that naturalised Germans; those engaged in certain trades necessary to this country; and those employing British labour are exempt from the order, which does not, meanwhile, apply to Austrians or Hungarians.'

While football matches were still being played in the city, the opportunity was taken to recruit young men from the crowd as reported in *The Daily Record*:

'At a meeting of the Footballers' Committee to assist in Army recruiting, held in the Grosvenor Restaurant, Glasgow, last night, under the chairmanship of Sir John Ure-Primrose, it was intimated that Councillor George T. Sampson would speak at Firhill Park this afternoon and that Councillor R. Hunter would render a similar service at Shawfield Park.

It was also reported that, so far, the results had been most gratifying. Quite a large number of men have been sent from the various football grounds to join well-known regiments, and many others have intimated their willingness to join the proposed football corps. Next week, every effort will be made to obtain fresh recruits.'

In the football section of the newspaper it was reported:

'If the War Office desire that football should cease, the English FA is prepared to see that the wish is carried out. Such, it may be taken for granted, is also the attitude of the Scottish FA. To the suggestion that players ought to enlist, it may be replied that professional

Wounded men recuperating in Strobhill Hospital in Glasgow. Several men took part in the great battle of the Aisne. The photo shows no fewer than ten regiments including the Scottish Rifles, the Scottish Fusiliers, the Sussex RFA, the Connaught Rangers, the Inniskilling Dragoons and the King's Own Yorkshire Regiment.

players are legally bound to their clubs. They are, therefore, not at liberty to enlist unless the clubs grant them release from their agreement.'

The Daily Record of Thursday 8 October carried an article about their appeal for blankets for troops:

'The appeal we made for blankets for our gallant and brave lads, who are filling the ranks, met with a splendid response. We call a halt now simply because the demand for the moment has been met.

Had it been necessary, there is not the slightest doubt that the generous-hearted public, who quite appreciate what are boys are doing for them at the front, would have contributed every blanket needed.

A good many blankets and other comfortable items, sent to the City Chambers, under care of the Lord Provost, Sir Daniel M. Stevenson, since the orders from headquarters at Stirling to cease collecting, will be carefully looked after. Our readers may rest assured that not one article sent there will go astray – not even the football which came along with some blankets from Selkirk.

Our intention is to confide all the blankets and other things, which have been coming flowing in even after the order to cease collecting blankets, to the Red Cross in Glasgow, who have been doing magnificent work, and under whose auspices contributors will be pleased to know that their gifts to Tommy Atkins will go directly to the front.'

Gaby Entwistle, a 3-year-old Belgian refugee, flying the flag in Glasgow on Saturday 3 October. A record amount of money was taken on Belgian Flag day with over 2,000,000 flags sold. Little Gaby encouraged buyers to purchase flags with some patrons paying £2 for them. The money went towards the Belgian Relief Fund.

On Wednesday 14 October, several hundred men of the Clyde Division of the Royal Naval Reserve Volunteers arrived in Glasgow after taking part in the defence of Antwerp. The men arrived at Dover on the previous Monday before travelling up to Glasgow on two special trains.

Their arrival in the city was unknown to the public until the men were spotted in the streets looking begrimed and wearing torn clothing. It was said that because of their dishevelled appearance, every man made his way to the hairdressers to make themselves look more presentable before heading to their homes. Many of the men belonged to the Greenock companies and they headed back home from the city in the late afternoon and evening.

When interviewed by *The Daily Record and Sunday Mail*, the men said that, as far as they knew, very few of the Scottish contingent had been killed, probably a dozen. However, sixty were wounded and over a hundred were missing. It was thought that the missing men had probably been captured by the Germans during the hurried evacuation of the city.

The Daily Record of 15 October reported on German espionage during the fight at Antwerp:

'Two A.B.'s of the Royal Naval Volunteer Reserve, who had fought side by side in the trenches, told a harrowing tale of the struggle in the city's suburbs, adding details of the enemy's espionage system which render the fancies of fiction writers almost crude by comparison.

They left one of the Kent coastal towns on the Sunday morning and sailed to Dunkirk whence they entrained to Antwerp. Arriving there on the Tuesday, they immediately set about the work of entrenching.

"It was hard, desperately hard, work," said the spokesman of the two. "We were at it incessantly, hour after hour, day and night, getting our quick-firers into position, piling up the sandbags and making everything secure against the overwhelmingly heavy cannonade which we knew, almost intuitively, we would have to face.

"When the attack came – well, I can hardly tell you what transpired. It was simply awful. What were our machine guns against the long range artillery of the Germans? But one thing I must say – it was a pretty long time before the Germans got our range. For a long, long time – I don't know how long, as time does not go by hours in modern warfare – their shells flew and screamed right over us, falling far behind. How they ultimately got our range, I don't know but I have my suspicions in view of what transpired."

"What was that?" asked our representative.

"Oh, just their spies. They were everywhere. But let me tell you

Two contingents, both of 200 men, from the Glasgow City Battalions had a route march through the city's streets on the afternoon of Friday 16 October. The men of the 1st Battalion can be seen wearing their tramway uniforms.

A sergeant with a section of Glasgow's Own parading in Glasgow on Friday 16 October.

this first. The shells gradually got our range, signalled, no doubt, by aeroplanes, too, in addition to the spies we afterwards discovered. Those aeroplanes were hovering everywhere over us and our lot at least could not bring them down, for we had no high-angle guns with us. When the shells came, we simply had to go. It was positive hell, one continuous shrieking rain of iron, which crumpled up our defences and compelled us to retire. What a time that was! We withdrew and after that were gradually driven along."

"Were you near Dutch territory at all during your retreat?"

"Yes, within three hundred yards, I believe. We just managed to keep on the right side. I suppose those now interned there never knew they had crossed the border line in the desperate nature of the struggle."

"And now, about those spies?" our representative asked.

"Why," replied the A.B., "you may scarcely believe this but they

The first contingent of 3,000 Belgian Refugees arriving in the city during October. The citizens of Glasgow gave them a warm welcome and they later had dinner at the City Hall.

were actually in the trenches with us. Some were wearing the uniforms of Belgian soldiers, some posed as civilian guides and, while actually plying us with chocolates, were ascertaining our every movement and were finding out all they possibly could about the disposal of our forces, their strength and their equipment.

"It was only when the retreat commenced that our suspicions became a grim certainty. Some of us were actually led within 300 yards of the German forces and but for the arrival of a genuine scout, I don't know what might have happened.

"Yes, I believe a number of those dirty fellows were caught afterwards and shot."

An advert appeared in *The Daily Record* of Saturday 24 October which appealed for volunteers to join the army. The advert read:

LORD KITCHENER'S ARMY.
1st AND 2nd GLASGOW BATTALIONS H.L.I.
A number of recruits are required to urgently complete these battalions. Enlistment for the 1st Battalion at 46 Bath Street and for the 2nd Battalion at St. Andrew's Halls, Kent Road, from 11 a.m. to 10 p.m.
D.M Stevenson, Lord Provost.

On 19 October, the First Battle of Ypres began.

The Daily Record of Tuesday 3 November carried news of a recent appeal for gifts for soldiers:

> 'In response to an appeal made from the pulpit of Langside Avenue United Free Church, Glasgow, some weeks ago, the ladies of the congregation have provided 330 pairs of socks, 108 body belts, 25 pairs of mittens, 16 helmets and 7 mufflers. These have been made up into three large bales and forwarded by Mrs Fairley to the headquarters in London.'

An advert in *The Daily Record* of Saturday 7 November appealed for young men to join the territorial force who, it said, were urgently required for foreign service. The advert said that it believed that the Lowland Division would be the first territorial force to serve overseas, as foreshadowed in the speech by Earl Kitchener in the House of Lords on 17 September. The unit were looking for men over 19 years old and many tradesmen were required, particularly shoeing smiths.

Adverts also appealed for men to join the Royal Naval Brigade to fight alongside Kitchener's New Army. No experience was necessary

Kitchener's recruitment poster, 'Your country needs you!' A huge recruitment campaign encouraged young men to join up. By January 1915, almost one million men had enlisted. Pals battalions encouraged many to enlist and they ultimately provided enough men for three battalions.

On Saturday 7 November, there was a march through Glasgow by the 7th Battalion Cameron Highlanders. The aim of the march was to boost recruitment. The photo shows Sergeant Adam and his pipers.

Great scenes of enthusiasm welcomed a contingent of 1,960 Belgians who had responded to the appeal of King Albert for volunteers for the Belgian Army. On Friday 13 November, the men marched from the Christian Institute to St Enoch Station. They were led by representatives of the Glasgow Corporation and by the Tramways Pipe Band.

and the minimum height for applicants was 5ft 3½ inches. Applicants were asked to report to the RNVR Headquarters at 52 Whitefield Road, Govan.

A letter appeared in *The Daily Record* of Tuesday 24 November which was sent by a Glasgow private in the Highland Light Infantry to a friend living in the city. It read:

'I am taking the chance of writing this during a lull in the fighting, for although this is Sunday, we cannot lay aside our arms – every day is practically alike here. My regiment is at present in the most advanced position of the field and has, for the past seven days, been continually keeping the Germans (who are entrenched about 150 to

A corporal in Lochiel's Cameron Highlanders encouraging men to enlist in George Square, Glasgow.

200 yards in front of us) in check. The enemy have tried to break through repeatedly by day and night but their favourite time seems to be just about dawn.

Two nights ago, there was a very thick mist and we could see only about five yards in front. The Germans, taking advantage of this, got very near before they started to charge our trenches. But our men opened a cross-fire on the Germans that must have cost the enemy a great many lives, as they always come in great numbers. As far as I know, we lost three killed and a few wounded but the heaps of Germans lying outside our trenches testified to the marksmanship of our men. We took sixty-one prisoners, who seemed to be glad to get caught.

Whether there is any truth in the statement they made to us, I can't say but, according to these statements, the last line of the German reserves had been called up. They stated that most of the Army Corps they belonged to were thoroughly disheartened and broken in spirit through an insufficiency of food, repeated repulses by our heavy fire and the lies that are being printed by the German newspapers about alleged successful advances and captures, which the men are beginning to see for themselves are untrue. They said that a great many of their men were waiting for the first chance to lay down their rifles and give themselves up as prisoners.

The most trying time that we have is just before an attack is made, as the enemy always shell our trenches for about half an hour before the charge takes place and it is just as if the gates of hell were opened on you. But the "Jack Johnsons" do very little real damage on account of the soft ground, unless you get in their way.

We had a good two hours of these yesterday, five of them landing near by, one going into a trench, but nobody was hurt. My trench was not touched being 100 yards behind, where we would have to cover a retreat or take part in a charge, as the case might be.'

A Glasgow surgeon, Lieutenant William Miller, was reported killed when HMS *Bulwark* exploded while anchored near Sheerness on 26 November. The explosion was thought to be caused by overheating of cordite charges near to the ship's boiler. The explosion resulted in the loss of 736 men. Of the fourteen survivors, two later died in hospital.

The Daily Record of Saturday 28 November reported that the 9th Battalion of the Highland Light Infantry (the Glasgow Highlanders) had

Under the headline 'Jocks cleaning up after a night in the trenches', this photo appeared in *The Daily Record* of Friday 4 December and was taken 'somewhere in France'. The caption read: 'When the Scottish troops have spent the night in the trenches, their first thought in the morning is to scrub their knees. Cleanliness with Jock is next to godliness always.'

The machine-gun section of the Glasgow Highlanders practising at Gailes. The gun is mounted on a carriage so that it can be easily moved about. *The Daily Record* stated: 'The men are fine types of sturdy Scots.'

been in action at the front. It was said that they formed part of the defensive line at Ypres. The paper reported:

'Cordial in the extreme was the send-off which the battalion received when, about a month ago, the men, mustering 1,000 strong, left, along with the 15th Cameronians, for the fighting line. The Highlanders presented a very fine appearance, for it is an open secret that only a superior type of young men was accepted when the foreign service battalion was being enrolled.

While enquiries in Glasgow last night failed to discover any direct confirmation

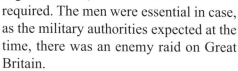

Tobacco Day on Saturday 12 December raised funds to supply pipes, tobacco and cigarettes to the soldiers at the front. Four young ladies can be seen selling flags on a cold windy day in Buchanan Street.

of the statement that the lads in the philabeg had been in action, letters received by relatives of members of the regiment yesterday indicate that if not actually engaged, when these were written, the battalion was then expecting to advance into the firing line.'

Towards the end of November, it was reported that there was a severe shortage of Territorials. In Glasgow alone 4,000 additional men were required. The men were essential in case, as the military authorities expected at the time, there was an enemy raid on Great Britain.

Despite the war, entertainment continued in the city and on 5 December, the Olympia at Bridgeton Cross, announced Glasgow's first pantomime of the season entitled 'Goody Two Shoes'.

A story appeared in *The Aberdeen Evening Express* of Saturday 19 December under the headline A BRAVE TRAMWAYMAN. It read:

Second Lieutenant Wilcox and some of the men of the 6th (Reserve) Battalion of the Highland Light Infantry. An appeal was launched in December for more men to join the kilted battalion.

Major Stewart, Colonel Meikle and Captain Scott of the 6th Highland Light Infantry. The regiment was commanded by Colonel Hugh D.P. Chalmers VD.

'A brave deed of a Glasgow soldier is recorded by Private Robert Bruce, of the 1st Battalion Gordon Highlanders, in a letter to friends in Govanhill. Private Bruce, who has been fighting in Belgium for five weeks, says:

"We have had a few stiff fights in that time. At Ypres, we gave the Germans more than they wanted. The British lines, as you know, could not be broken, and we fairly hurled our troops against the famous Prussian Guard, who were terribly cut up. On November 15, the Germans made a terrible attack on our lines. It was during the night, their favourite time for attacking. Our rifles blazed out a continuous and solid fire. They had advanced to our barbed wire but past that they could not get, as our fire swept the field. Next morning, at grey dawn, from among the pile of German dead, could be heard a groan. Our boys shouted 'Come in, old chap', but he could only rise on his elbow and groan. At this point, Sergeant James

The Five Brewster Girls, an English dancing troupe, appeared in Glasgow in December. They had previously been detained in Hamburg for two months as prisoners of war.

Harry Lauder and his wife at the Central Station in Glasgow in December on their way home to Dunoon after an extensive world tour.

McKenna, of 'A' Company, volunteered to go out and fetch him in, which he did under fire of the enemy. The German's shoulder was shattered. He was one of the Prussian Guard. It is here I'm glad to mention that Govanhill claims the hero of that incident, as Sergeant McKenna who resides at 284 Calder Street. He was employed as a car driver on the Glasgow cars and was stationed at Langside depot.'"

On 22 December, the Scottish Football Association Council decreed at their meeting in Glasgow that there would be no Scottish Cup ties this

Belgian refugee children were presented with Christmas gifts in Glasgow during December. The gifts were generously donated by the children of the United Stated of America. The presentation was organised through the Corporation of Glasgow Belgian Refugees' Committee. The children are pictured with Mrs Alexander Walker and Mrs James Stewart.

season. They said that they were duty bound not to proceed with their National Cup competitions after the War Office requested that no cup-ties or international matches should be played this season. Mr H.J. Tennant said at the meeting that he thought that football should be stopped altogether. This comment was seconded by Mr W. McIntosh.

At the front, on 24 December, an unofficial Christmas truce was observed.

In *The Hamilton Advertiser* of Saturday 26 December, the main pantomime for the Christmas period was mentioned:

'The pantomime season opened at the Theatre Royal, Glasgow, last Thursday evening, when Howard & Wyndham's twenty-seventh Royal pantomime, "Little Miss Muffet", was most successfully produced. The "book" is written by Mr J. James Hewson and the production is presented in a series of bright and beautiful stage pictures which more than maintain, and go far to enhance, the tradition of the Theatre Royal for opulent splendour in its pantomime productions. While the pantomime as a vaudeville entertainment takes high rank in the record of "Royal" productions, the nursery note is commendably accentuated. A splendid company has been arranged for the presentation of "Miss Muffet". Place of honour falls to Miss Maie Ash, who in the title role at once established a most favourable impression. Miss Ash is to be complimented on her unquestioned success. Besides having considerable powers as a comedienne and considerable skill as a pleasing vocalist, Miss Ash has histrionic gift which even in pantomime production shines through. Miss Nancy Langtyre makes a handsome and dashing "principal boy". The costumes, as usual, are the last word in opulence. The succession of beautiful stage pictures unfolded, particularly in "Spiderland",

Miss Maie Ash who appeared in Little Miss Muffet at the Theatre Royal, Glasgow during December. According to *The Daily Record*: 'Miss Ash is to be complimented on her unquestioned success. Besides having considerable powers as a comedienne and considerable skill as a pleasing vocalist, Miss Ash has histrionic gift which even in pantomime production shines through.'

calls for enthusiastic commendation. Mr Harry Ashton, the popular manager, succeeded in comfortably placing an audience which completely filled the house.'

On 29 December, at Greenock Sheriff Court, Sir John Harvard Biles of Wemyss Bay was charged with failing to provide details of aliens who were in his service. One of the aliens, a Norwegian, was also charged with failing to register with the proper authorities. A plea of guilty was accepted in both cases and it was acknowledged that the matter had been an oversight. Sheriff Welsh gave an admonition in both cases.

At the end of December, a letter was received by Mrs Bruce of 10 Jamieson Street, Govanhill, informing her that her husband, Private Robert T. Bruce, of the Gordon Highlanders, had been killed in action in Belgium.

The letter read: 'We were in the trenches from the 18th till the 21st, and it was on the 19th that Private Bruce got shot clean through the head. Although he lived about an hour, he suffered no pain.'

Private Bruce was 28 years old when he died and was well-known in the Govanhill district where he acted as honorary secretary to the local Unionist Association. He was formerly employed in the warehouse of Messrs Mair, Clark and McLean.

Chapter Two

1915 – Deepening Conflict

New Year's Day was welcomed in by wretched weather, as mentioned in *The Daily Record* of Saturday 2 January:

> To the disappointment of holiday-makers in Glasgow yesterday, the weather, which on the previous day gave such promise of excellent behaviour, broke down. Even a covering of snow on the pavements might have been less unwelcome than the rain. Its comparative novelty would have made amends to some extent for any discomfort experienced.
>
> With the rain came squalls of wind, which accentuated the worries of those who ventured abroad, and the task of keeping umbrellas turning inside out, and from starting off upon a trip of their own account, was not an easy one. Hats made many sportive journeys and always sought the muddiest place in which to await the arrival of the exasperated pursuer.

Four members of Lochiel's Camerons on furlough in Glasgow. The men shown are Alick Logan, Andrew Fraser, J.R. Armstrong and Guy Logan. They received military training at Aldershot and were members of C Company's crack football team.

Tempers, New Year resolutions notwithstanding, were sadly ruffled by the weather vagaries.

Indoors became imperative for those who desired to spend the holiday in comfort. Family parties were numerous, but everybody in Glasgow had not arranged to meet round the social table. For such the picture houses, music-halls and theatres, with which the city is so liberally provided, promised relief from tedium. Crowded houses resulted and many failed to gain admission.

Business was generally suspended. The shopkeeping section of the community, whose opportunities for participating in the delights of holiday-making are not plentiful, made the most of the occasion.'

Also, on 1 January, the Admiralty announced, through the Press Bureau, the capture of the German cruiser *Emden* by HMS *Sydney*. The report stated that the Germans had put up a poor fight.

On 8 January, a promenade concert was held by the 7th Cameronians at their headquarters to encourage recruitment. A dance was held afterwards. Similar functions took place elsewhere throughout the week and recruitment in the city was said to be 'booming'.

A long list of of casualties, including both officers and men of the BEF was issued by the press bureau in January. It included the names of

The 5th Cameronians and the 9th Highland Light Infantry (Glasgow Highlanders) left the city on Thursday 14 January and received a tremendous send-off with crowds cheering them on their way. The photo shows the Glasgow Highlanders marching to St Andrew's Hall where they were the guests of Glasgow Corporation.

many Scottish men from the Gordon Highlanders, the Highland Light Infantry and the Royal Scots Fusiliers.

In the House of Lords, in reply to a question by Lord Moncrieff, Lord Lucas stated that the drab kilts that were being issued to Scottish regiments was only a temporary measure because a sufficient number of tartan kilts couldn't be supplied in time.

During January, the War Office invited Glasgow to raise a city Army Corps, known as Glasgow's Own, adding to the three battalions of infantry already in training. The corps would comprise both an artillery and an engineering unit. The corporation said that they were delighted to be taking part and felt that the enthusiasm of the city would soon be behind the idea. They stated that they were already proud that the *Tiger, New Zealand* and *Indomitable* had been built on the Clyde and that a huge force of engineers was available to join the corps, although it wasn't their desire to take men who were already employed doing vital government work. The hope was to recruit a gun brigade of four batteries with twenty-two officers and 646 men. The reserve would consist of twenty-two officers and seventy-two men. There was also to be a company of engineers consisting of six officers and 230 men, with the reserve consisting of seventy-five men.

The Daily Record of Saturday 30 January reported on the hearty send-off for the reserve battalions of the Cameronians:

'Enthusiastic scenes were witnessed yesterday afternoon when a draft of the 7th Cameronians Reserve Battalion left Glasgow to join the regiment at their own station in Scotland. In a way the demonstrations were reminiscent of those which took place a week ago when the 2nd Glasgow Battalion marched through the city.

The members of the draft paraded at the Regimental headquarters, Coplaw Street, off Victoria Road. They were dressed in full marching order, minus greatcoats, and presented a fine appearance. The whole of the remainder of the reserve battalion turned out along with the regimental band and pipers and accompanied the draft to the station.

With the bands alternately playing stirring tunes, the column proceeded to Queen Street Station by way of Victoria Road, Eglinton Street, Jamaica Street, Union Street, Renfield Street, St Vincent Street and Queen Street to the station. At various points, large crowds had gathered and the troops were frequently cheered.

On the platform of the station, the Reserve Battalion was drawn up and as the train departed, the brass band played "Tipperary",

The funeral of Sergeant Major Uphill and his daughter took place in Glasgow towards the end of January. Both had been killed in a motor accident in the city. A large crowd gathered to watch the procession and to pay their respects.

while the troops cheered their comrades of the draft enthusiastically. The site was quite an inspiring one.

After the draft had left, the battalion had a short route march through the city.'

On 6 February, *The Daily Record* reported that one of its former workers, Harry McCartney, had been killed while serving with the 1st Cameron Highlanders. His battalion had been engaged in the heavy fighting at La Bassée where he met his death at 19 years old. Friends and colleagues described him as 'a bright and intelligent lad, whose cheery disposition endeared him to all with whom he came in contact'.

Private McCartney was the second member of the staff of *The Daily Record* to be killed in action. The first, Corporal Fred Carpenter, died in the early part of November 1914.

A group of men from the Second Battalion of the 5th Cameronians receiving instruction in the art of trench digging before leaving to fight in France.

An advert appeared for recruits for the 6th (Reserve) Battalion of the Highland Light Infantry in *The Daily Record* of Saturday 13 February. It read:

'A few recruits, of good character and physique, age 19 to 35 years, are required to complete the establishment of the regiment. Recruits must enlist for foreign service and will be discharged at the end of the war. Recruits will be enlisted daily from 9am till 9pm and will receive an immediate issue of clothing.'

'THIS BATTALION WEARS THE KILT.'

On 15 February, at the annual meeting of John Watson Ltd in Glasgow, Mr John Strain, the chairman, said that with the Great War raging and the consequence of trade disturbances, the company's coal output and profit had diminished considerably.

One of their directors, Mr H.L. Strain, stated that about 600 of their employees had left the company to join His Majesty's forces which left them with an eleven per cent net shortage of workers. This left them with a decrease of over 100,000 tons in output during 1914.

The company stated that the problems mentioned had led to a shortage of fuel and high prices which, they felt, could only be relieved

The pipe band of the 8th Cameronians marched through Alexandra Parade after a morning of trench digging in a field in the neighbourhood of Cumbernauld Road in January. The pipe music was said to have inspired recruiting.

by the temporary suspension of the Miners' Eight Hours Act and by allowing work to proceed on Sundays.

On 19 February, the Dardanelles Campaign began.

The Daily Record of Monday 22 February reported on the recruiting efforts in the city:

'Special efforts are to be made this week in Glasgow to stimulate recruiting by enlisting the services of every soldier to act more or less as a Recruiting Sergeant.

A pair of theatre tickets will be the reward given to each soldier who secures at least one recruit during the week. As an extra incentive, some of the commanding officers will offer an extra half-holiday to the members of their battalion successful in earning the theatre tickets.Recruits may be enlisted at the various drill halls, the Gallowgate office or at the rooms reserved at the Pavilion for recruiting purposes this week.

As already announced, the Harry Lauder Pipe Band will march through the streets of Glasgow with local battalions each day this week, and will appear at the Pavilion each evening.

Motor car drivers, electricians with magnetic experience and blacksmiths are wanted immediately for military service. Remuneration for these trades is at the rate of 6s a day, all found, with special separation allowance.

Captain George Mason, Mechanical Transport, ASC, will be present this week at the Pavilion recruiting office and will be pleased to interview applicants. It is particularly requested, however, that only those with very good experience should apply.

Tomorrow afternoon, at two o'clock, a short recruiting march by the 7th (Reserve) Battalion of the HLI, headed by the Harry Lauder Pipe Band, will take place in the neighbouring district of the city. On Friday evening a theatre night will be held at the Princess's Theatre, when members of the Battalion will be admitted in uniform, with their friends, at half price to all parts of the house.

In addition to the appearance of Harry Lauder's Pipe Band, it has been arranged that the pipe band of the Cameron Highlanders will visit the city this week to stimulate the recruiting for this popular regiment. The Camerons have proved themselves one of the most efficient regiments in the service and a very large proportion of the new battalions have been recruited in Glasgow, including the Stock Exchange and University contingents.'

During the week ending 10 March, the roll of the Glasgow Reserve Units of the Territorial Force was increased by 100 compared with 139 for the previous week. At the Gallowgate recruiting headquarters, an additional 525 men had enlisted during the week.

On 11 March, ballot papers were issued to Clyde engineers asking if they agreed for their wages claim to be taken to arbitration. The engineers had requested a wage increase of another halfpenny per hour saying that, because of the war, trade was exceptionally busy at the moment.

The ballot papers were issued to forty-nine branches affected by the claim and the Glasgow District Committee recommended that the men vote in favour of arbitration.

On Thursday 12 March, a meeting of the corporation in Glasgow read out a letter received from Colonel Donald J. Mackintosh, the assistant director of medical services. It suggested that the Kelvingrove Art Galleries should be utilized as a military hospital containing 520 beds. He explained that the building could be used as a hospital with no alteration to its structure and that he would have not made the request had the building not been exceptionally suited for use as a hospital. He knew of no other public building within the city that could be so easily adapted for the purpose.

The committee agreed to recommend that the request be acceded to. Mr Steele commented that they were in the midst of one of the most strenuous times that the country had ever experienced. Unfortunately, many men were returning home wounded and it was necessary to make adequate provision for them.

The story of a German submarine's attack on a Glasgow ship was reported in *The Daily Record* of Thursday 18 March:

'The attempted scuttling of Messrs J. & P. Hutchison's Glasgow steamer, *Atalanta*, 519 tons, by the crew of a German submarine off Inishturk, on the West Coast of Ireland on Sunday morning, presents features of new interest in so far that a gunfire attack was made on the crew of the steamer and a serious effort was made by the Germans to shoot the captain and men before scuttling the ship.

It is presumed that either the submarine's stock of torpedoes was exhausted or that the commander did not care to waste £1,000 worth of torpedo on the steamer when less valuable destructive material could be used with an equal result.

The *Atalanta* left Galway on Sunday morning at four o'clock with a general cargo for Glasgow, and while proceeding in a north-west direction, about nine miles west of Inishturk, a submarine was sighted from the stern of the steamer.

When first seen, at about ten o'clock, the submarine was about 6 miles away and the officers of the vessel had some doubt as to her nationality. At the same time nothing was left to chance and Captain McLarnon ordered the engineers to drive the ship at its best speed.

The German craft, however, which was not submerged, was capable of a greater speed and a very unequal race, lasting about an hour, resulted in the submarine coming almost abeam of the Glasgow vessel, with about half-a-dozen of her crew surrounding the turret. The sea was calm but apparently the steamer was not in hailing distance and, as a signal to her to stop, three rockets were fired across the deck.

Captain McLarnon paid no attention to the signals. The German then hoisted his ensign and, manning a machine gun at the bow of the submarine, fired a shell at the steamer.

Not satisfied with attempting to sink the ship with all hands on board, the submarine commander evidently ordered members of his crew to use guns and revolvers with the object of picking off anyone on the steamer who attempted to enter the lifeboats or showed himself in any way.

But the Germans had to deal with a cool and resourceful captain and crew. Exposing one side of his ship to the submarine, Captain McLarnon ordered the boats to quietly be lowered on the opposite side. The lifeboat on the side next to the submarine had been already rendered useless by a shell.

The lowering of the lifeboats was quickly accomplished and one member of the crew ran the gauntlet of the Germans' rifle fire in order to provide himself with an overcoat and other clothes which he'd left behind in the forecastle. When the German commander saw the crew rowing away for their lives towards Inishturk, he ran up alongside the steamer and sent his men on board with a bomb to blow her up.

When last seen by her captain and crew, the *Atalanta* was on fire, the result of the explosion of the bomb. The lifeboats, after a hard, exhausting pull, reached Inishturk, where they were heartily welcomed by the few natives of the island and afterwards covered another 15 miles in rowing to the mainland and eventually arrived in Glasgow yesterday.'

Also on 18 March, the Glasgow steamer, *Glenartney*, which was travelling from Bangkok to London with a cargo of rice, was torpedoed near the *Sovereign Lightship II*. The captain and 41 of the crew landed at Newhaven. An apprentice drowned and the steamer sank within half an hour.

On the morning of Tuesday 22 March, 100 wounded men arrived at the Royal Infirmary in Glasgow straight from Neuve Chapelle. The wounded included men from many Scottish regiments including the Argyll and Sutherland Highlanders, the Black Watch, the Scots Guards, the Cameron Highlanders, the Gordon Highlanders, the Seaforth Highlanders, the Royal Scots Fusiliers, the Royal Scots, the Cameronians, the Highland Light Infantry and the King's Own Scottish Borderers.

On Tuesday 13 April, some of the crew from the torpedoed Glasgow

**Female carriage cleaners at Glasgow's Central Station who were
employed to replace the men who had left to enlist. Their forewoman was
Mrs Anderson who can be seen in white overalls to the right of the first
picture.**

steamer *President* returned to the city. The steamer had been torpedoed
off the Lizard by a submarine while on its way from the Clyde to St
Malo in France.

When the steamer was approached, an officer on board the German
submarine shouted to the crew, 'Take to the boats and be quick about it.'
The submarine's commander demanded the ship's papers but once on
board was quite apologetic and said to the captain, 'I am very sorry,
captain, but this is war.' Three of the German officers spoke English and
it was said that although they were brusque, they were not rude.

The crew were taken on board the submarine and an attempt to blow
the steamer up was made but failed. The men were handed over to an
English smack and the Germans returned to finish the job. The crew
were later picked up by a British destroyer before being landed at
Devonport.

**At the Second Battle of Ypres, beginning on 22 April, the Germans
used poison gas for the first time**.

A report in *The Daily Record* of Saturday 24 April stated that Glasgow
had collected a total of £4,600 during the recent Serbia Day. Half of the
proceeds were to be given to the Serbian Relief Fund while the other

half was donated to the Scottish Women's Hospital at Kragujevatz in Serbia.

On 25 April, the Battle of Gallipoli began.

Towards the end of April, arrangements were made in case of a possible aerial attack on the city. A report said that street lights should be lowered or extinguished together with lighting from factories and engineering works where work was carried on at night. Lights from shops, houses or illuminated signs were also to be reduced. *The Daily Record* reported:

'Viewed from a height overlooking the city, the street lights clearly show the city area, certain parts of the city being conspicuous. The principal streets, the harbour and the bridges over the Clyde can readily be defined. The orange-coloured electric lights in use in

A group of soldiers, all from the 1/5th Cameronians, who were recovering from wounds during May. Included in the photo is Private G. Wallace who was the first Glasgow Territorial to be wounded in the war. He can be seen 4th from the left in the back row.

certain streets show conspicuously in double or single lines. The lights on the waterfront show strongly by reflection.

A hostile aviator acquainted with the city, or having a good map, could identify the principal streets and in this way could fix the location of places which he decided to destroy. It is therefore necessary, for safety that on the alarm of hostile aircraft, all street lights should be extinguished.

There are about 500 miles of streets in the city lighted by 28,200 lights. At the present time, 17,450 lights are in use; 1600 of these are electric lights. The Inspector of Lighting has made arrangements by which the street lighting can be wholly extinguished within thirty minutes from the time of receiving intimation.'

On Sunday 2 May, a hospital train arrived from Southampton late at night with 103 wounded soldiers bound for Stobhill. Altogether, there were fifty stretcher cases. There were several men from the 7th Battalion Argyll and Sutherland Highlanders who had suffered terribly at Ypres. One member of the 7th stated that they had no fewer than 500 casualties which amounted to half of the battalion. They were at the front for five months and it was the first time that they had been in action.

The Daily Record reported on the wounded men:

'Sad cases were, of course, common. One of the most pathetic figures was Sergeant Eastwood, a burly member of the 5th Yorks. Despite the time which had elapsed since his removal from the fighting zone, the gallant Sergeant was still suffering severely.

Propped up in bed, and tended carefully by the gentle ward sister, he looked the gratitude his breathlessness would scarce permit him to speak.

"It's the cough I'm afraid of," he explained with an apologetic smile, when, in a respite from his agony, the Sergeant gave utterance to his thanks.

Across the ward, and comfortably tucked in by the kindly hands of his nurse, lay Private Thomas Buckley, of the 1st Battalion Warwicks. Like Sergeant Eastwood, this young soldier – he is but 18 years of age – had undergone a similar experience.

Relating his story, Private Buckley said that the Warwicks' position was shelled for two days and nights. When they thought sufficient damage had been done, and it was heavy enough in all conscience, the Germans began to send the poisonous fumes across towards the British lines. At that moment, reinforcements were on

Lord Provost Dunlop inspecting two battalions of Glasgow's Own (15th and 16th Highland Light Infantry) at Gailes camp during May. The Lord Provost can be seen saluting the men as they march by. The 15th Battalion was also known as the Tramway Battalion and the 16th as the Boys' Brigade Battalion.

the way to the Warwicks. The heavy vapour found its way among the men – those who had been on the spot doing "their bit" in the soldier's phrase – and the men who were coming up to lend their help. Like flies, they began to fall around him. The vapour choked and blinded them.'

Lieutenant Robert Rodger Glen of the Queen's Own Glasgow Yeomanry after his marriage to Miss Doreen Leigh-King during May.

On 7 May, the ocean liner RMS *Lusitania* was sunk by a German U-boat leading to the deaths of 1,198 of whom 128 were Americans. The sinking enraged the Americans and hastened their entry into the war.

News arrived in Glasgow of the death of Lieutenant R.H.A. Anderson of the 2nd Cameron Highlanders. He had been killed while in battle at Hill 60 on 12 May. He was 23 when he died and was the son of Mr A.C. Anderson, a stockbroker, of Buchanan Street, Glasgow.

He was stationed with his regiment in India at the outbreak of war before being sent to the Western Front. There, he was severely frost bitten and was invalided home. He recovered and was sent back to the front but died a few weeks later.

On Saturday 15 May, a Glasgow woman was killed when she was knocked down in the city. Mrs Shaw, of 60 Great Western Road, was stepping off a tramcar when she was hit by a van in Bothwell Street. The driver of the van was detained pending further investigation.

In the early hours of Monday 17 May, the Anchor-Cunarder *Transylvania* arrived safely in the Clyde from New York. Many passengers had received letters warning them not to travel as it was likely that the liner would be torpedoed. There was much relief when she docked without problem.

James McTague, a private in the Cameronians, admitted assaulting a comrade at the Drill Hall in Cathedral Street on 18 May by kicking and stabbing him. Mr D. Stevenson, Depute Fiscal, stated that while McTague was a prisoner in the guardroom, he broke out and attempted to escape. The complainer had assisted in getting him locked up and was kicked by the prisoner. Later, on the same day, McTague rushed from the ranks and stabbed the complainer on the right breast. McTague said that he had no recollection of the affair.

The sheriff, at the Glasgow Criminal Court, sent the accused to prison for six months.

On Thursday 27 May, *The Daily Record* carried an article under the headline NEED FOR MORE MEN. It read:

'Among the wounded brought to Strobhill Hospital on Saturday were several Glasgow Territorials. Private A.W. Gardner, 9th HLI (Glasgow Highlanders), who is wounded severely in the thigh, spoke of his experiences in the recent fierce fighting in the neighbourhood of La Bassée.

On Saturday, May 15th, the Highlanders supported the

Worcesters in an attempt to capture a line of trenches. This proved unsuccessful and later, they joined the 2nd HLI in trenches which had been captured by the Oxfords, the Bucks [sic] and the Inniskillings, and on Sunday rushed successfully some trenches of the enemy.

The shell fire of the Germans, he stated, was tremendous. They certainly did not suffer from any lack of shells. Our losses were very severe. When our men were wounded, there was no hope of getting them back as the Germans were attacking our communication trenches. A large number of stretcher-bearers were killed.

The enemy entrenchments at this place (Reichbourg) were a veritable stronghold – from 12 to 15 feet high of solid concrete. They had six months to prepare the place and had brought cart loads of cement from Antwerp. The Germans could live in such trenches with 6-inch howitzers playing all about them. Their guns, placed for deadly "ground firing", protruded through the cement almost on a level with the ground.

Private Gardner is a Glasgow man. Although he was living in London when war was declared, he made from there to join the Glasgow Highlanders. He was wounded by shrapnel while carrying a despatch to his Colonel. A portion of the muscle of his thigh is shot away and it is feared that he may have a permanent limp.

He thinks the young men of Scotland don't fully realise "what the war means out there". He is by no means cock-sure that the Allies are going to win and has much to say regarding the efficiency of the German army as a fighting machine.

Commenting on the gigantic nature of the task in front of the Allies and of the slowness of progress of any kind, he emphasises the fact that he had himself been in the "same line of trenches all the time since Christmas".'

Men of the 3rd Glasgow Highlanders being waved off by their loved ones. They left from Buchanan Street station on Saturday 29 May.

The Port Glasgow and Greenock Tramway Company followed the lead of Glasgow in June and introduced women conductors to their cars in order to release young men so that they could enlist in the army or navy. The photo shows the chief inspector and four lady pupil conductors.

At the beginning of June, an offer of a large first-line military hospital of 700 beds, made by the executive of the Scottish branch of the Red Cross Society, was accepted by the Director General of the Medical Service. He stated that it would be of great use and they would be very glad to have it.

The proposal was for the new hospital to be erected at Bellahouston

A group of highland dancers taking part in an open-air fete in Queen's Park, Glasgow during June. The money raised went towards the funds of the Scottish Branch of the British Red Cross Society.

In June, the Apex taxi-cab company in Glasgow hired two women drivers to replace the men who had left their jobs to enlist. A sign on the front of the cab encourages men to do their duty.

Park in Glasgow with a frontage near Paisley Road. It was felt that the park offered an ideal site with agreeable surroundings and fresh air while being easily accessible from the railway station. The suggested buildings were seven in number which were to be divided into wards of fifty beds each.

A new auxiliary hospital was also soon to be opened in Park Avenue in premises which were originally built to house the Glasgow and West of Scotland College of Domestic Science.

The Daily Record of Monday 21 June reported on some of the work done by women within the city:

'Owing to the number of Glasgow Corporation Lighting Department employees who have enlisted, several women have been engaged as stair lamplighters in the Eastern, Springburn and Govan districts. So satisfactorily have they performed their duties that it is proposed to extend the system to other parts of the city. The women receive the same pay at the start as the minimum wage of the men.'

Towards the end of June, the Glasgow and West of Scotland Armaments Committee announced that there was a keen interest in the Clyde area in Lloyd George's appeal for a volunteer army of munitions workers to be steadily built up.

Between 8,000 and 9,000 citizens employed on Clydeside had already signified their willingness to undertake war work whenever their services might be required. The result was achieved by an appeal by the Armaments Committee for volunteers to form a 'flying column' of 6,500 skilled workers. It was stipulated that the men must be employed in certain trades and not already involved in war work. They were promised wages equivalent to what they were currently earning.

On Wednesday 7 July, a complaint was made to the Hampstead

On the night of Thursday 3 June, before they left to enlist, the Italians in Glasgow held a patriotic demonstration. They were preceded by a brass band as they marched through the principal streets of the city after holding a meeting at George Square. The photo was taken at the base of the Queen Victoria statue.

magistrate by Mr Abraham Rosenthal about two visits he had received from a police officer. Mr Rosenthal was well known to the people of Glasgow and had aspired to parliamentary honours in the city several years previously.

It had been suggested that he was a German but he wanted to put the record straight by saying that he 'had not a drop of German blood in his veins'. He was a Jew and had been born in Scotland. On account of his name sounding German, he changed it to Abraham Montefiore, which was his wife's family name. He said that he had announced his change of name in an advertisement and did not think that the second visit from a police officer was warranted. Sub-Divisional Inspector Parker said that the second visit was due to the change of name after an inquiry by the postmaster general.

The magistrate said that the police had only carried out their duty but he sympathised with the complainant.

An advert appeared in the public notices section of *The Daily Record* of Thursday 8 July. It appealed for 10,000 men to join the Glasgow Territorial Force, Third Line.

At the beginning of July, foodstuffs intended for Germany, but captured by the British fleet, were put up for auction in Glasgow. The prize cargoes consisted of 1,700 boxes of meat, a large quantity of lard, several hundred 'tierees' of beef, as well as over 500 cases of ship's biscuits, over 100 bags of coffee beans and 250 bags of cocoa beans.

The articles, when captured, were being conveyed from America to Gothenburg. The goods were sold by public auction in the Trades Hall, Glassford Street at one o'clock on 8 July by Messrs Churchill and Sim of London on behalf of the Marshal of the Admiralty.

On Saturday 17 July, all the outgoing trains from Glasgow were crowded with people celebrating the Fair Holiday. At Queen Street and Buchanan Street stations, people boarded the trains for destinations all over Scotland and further into England.

Although there were six fewer steamers at the Broomielaw than there were in the previous year, twice as many passengers travelled on them than on the Fair Saturday the year before. Altogether, the number of passengers for the day totalled 8,000.

There was a great rush to get away from the Broomielaw but by eleven o'clock, the steamers were full and crowds poured back into Jamaica Street. Many made their way to the train station to get a

On Saturday 31 July, Private Henry May VC, arrived back in Glasgow to a tremendous welcome. When his train pulled up at Central Station, there were loud cheers from the people waiting there to see him. Many men carried him shoulder high through the streets. The photo shows Private May with his parents and brother.

Five sergeants of the Cameronians, together with Mr J.W. Handford of Gourock, performed amusing sketches at the Glenpark Gala during August. The money raised went to help the dependants of the men killed in the war.

connection to the coast. Those who had to remain in the city formed picnic parties to Rouken Glen and the Cathkin Braes.

The Ayreshire coast had a higher than normal amount of visitors because of the disinclination to cross the water to Arran or Rothesay because of Admiralty restrictions. Gourock Pier lacked the usual crowd, but Wemyss Bay, which served Rothesay and Campbell Town, had a great rush of passengers.

The Edinburgh Evening News of Friday 30 July 1915 reported:

'The cloth cap hitherto worn by the women conductors on the Glasgow Corporation tramways cars has been replaced by a hat made of dark green straw trimmed with ribbon to match. The conductor's badge and number are fastened in front. The hats were handed out yesterday when the women went on duty. There are now nearly 700 women acting as conductors.'

Private Henry May VC, raised above the shoulders of well-wishers when he returned to Glasgow at the end of July.

The crowds waiting to welcome Private Henry May VC back to Glasgow on 31 July.

The Daily Record of Tuesday 3 August carried news of the severe Scottish losses in the Dardanelles. Many regiments, including the 7th and 8th Cameronians (Glasgow Territorials), the 4th Royal Scots (Queen's Edinburgh), the 7th Royal Scots (Leith Territorials) and the 5th Royal Scots Fusiliers (Ayr Territorials) suffered greatly with many men reported missing, wounded or killed. The newspaper contained long lists of the names of men affected.

Drilling was resumed by the various companies of the Glasgow Training Force after having been suspended during the Glasgow Fair Holidays. The official inspection of the force was due to take place the following month by Colonel Newbigging, a representative of the War Office for the Scottish Volunteer Association.

On Monday 9 August, at the County Buildings in Glasgow, a General Munitions Tribunal was held to deal with the case of thirty men employed by Messrs Lobnitz & Co, engineers and shipbuilders of Renfrew. It was alleged that the men had left their positions and taken part in a strike in contravention of Section 2 of the Munitions of War Act and that they remained on strike from Friday 30 July until Monday 2 August.

Lord Provost Dunlop inspecting detachments from three Glasgow territorial regiments in George Square on Thursday 26 August.

Mr Frank Gillon, the assistant foreman, said that he had appealed to the men not to strike on patriotic grounds but his pleas were ignored. Asked if he had definite instructions to not let the men out, he replied that he had but added, 'You might as well try and stop a regiment of Germans as to stop these men.'

Professor Gload, presiding, found that twenty-eight, out of the thirty

Men of the Glasgow Highlanders and the Camerons prepare for dinner in the trenches 'somewhere in France' during September.

A photo of the Glasgow Highlanders in the trenches in France during September.

On Wednesday 1 September, the Glasgow Flower Show was held in aid of the Red Cross and War Fund. There was a large attendance at the annual exhibition at the Glasgow and West of Scotland Horticultural Society which was held in the Exhibition Hall, New City Road.

workmen present, were guilty as charged. He fined the men 5 shillings each with the alternative of five days' imprisonment.

The Daily Record of Saturday 21 August carried a story of a wager that resulted in two youths being arrested:

> 'In Glasgow Marine Police Court yesterday, two youths were charged with committing a breach of the harbour regulations by swimming at the point where the Kelvin joins the Clyde at Partick. It transpired that they decided, for a wager, to swim from one bank to the other and back again, and in this they were successful. The charge to which they pleaded guilty had not been made for over twenty years.
>
> Bailie Irwin admonished the accused and characterised their feat as emblematic of British pluck.'

At the beginning of September, it was reported by the Chief Constable of Glasgow that there were 113 fewer cases of drunkenness in the previous week with the introduction of the new Liquor Control Regulations.

On 5 September, Tsar Nicholas II took control of Russia's armies.

The Evening Despatch of Monday 13 September reported the story of a soldier shot in the city:

> 'A singular shooting accident occurred in Glasgow on Saturday night.

Private James Quinn, a soldier home on furlough, was alighting from a tramcar with his rifle, when the weapon suddenly discharged and the shot entered the lower part of the body of another soldier on leave, Private Simon Lawson, who was walking along the street.

After passing through his body, the bullet broke the plate-glass window of a shop. Lawson succumbed to his injuries several hours after admission to the infirmary. Quinn was detained by the police.'

The death of a Glasgow Highlander was reported in *The Daily Record* during September. Lance Corporal Jas. Sydney Kerr was killed in action in France on 21 September by shell fire. He was 19 years old and had served with the Glasgow Highlanders for two and a half years. He was the only son of Mr and Mrs Robert Kerr of Gibson Street, Hillhead, Glasgow. Before enlisting, he was employed by Mr Easton, a stockbroker in Glasgow. Formerly, he had been a staff sergeant in the 28th Company Boys' Brigade in Hillhead.

The Daily Record of Tuesday 28 September reported on a Glasgow invasion of Paisley:

'It is some years since Paisley suffered as it did last night from an invasion of Glasgow drouths'.

The fine weather brought large numbers of respectable holiday-makers to the town during the day and though the streets were crowded, good order prevailed and little drunkenness was observed. In the evening, however, the scene was changed. The rapid service of tramway cars brought to the Cross large crowds and many of the visitors appeared to make for the public houses which were soon thronged by thirsty Glaswegians.

As each car was emptied, it was filled by returning holiday makers and for hours, the wide area at the Cross was occupied by an assemblage of at least 2,000 people, most of whom were waiting to get away.

The scene was a very animated one and the police, who were on duty in considerable numbers, had a lot to do in maintaining the regular street traffic and taking care of incapables. That these were numerous is evidenced by the fact that from 5.15 until ten o'clock over fifty apprehensions had been made. The accommodation at the police station was fully taxed, sixty persons being given night quarters.

The public-houses in the centre of the town were closed at a quarter to nine o'clock.'

On 1 October, as a prelude to the next day's march, a concert was held at the headquarters of the 7th Cameronians at Coplawhill in Glasgow. Mr Harry Lauder and other artistes from various music halls gave their services. At the concert, Sir Samuel Chisholm said:

'The time has come when shirkers must be hunted out of their corners. It must be brought home to them that there is a duty lying on their shoulders which in the sight of God and man they must perform. Otherwise they are covering themselves with shame present and shame eternal. I wish that I could get at the heart of a man who is of age and who circumstances permit who has not offered himself.

Such a man is a coward. He is acting the part of a coward and there is no room for cowards in days such as these. It was not a pack of cowards who rushed on the German trenches on Saturday and Sunday and Monday last. They were men who Glasgow has great reason to be proud of; and although we have to lament the loss of many dear and precious lives, the men who have fallen have sent their names through years, ay, I may say, generations to come as having taken part, and a glorious part, in this great conflict, the result of which will either establish or destroy the fabric of our national freedom and the fabric of the world's civilization. So come forward and do your duty.'

After performing two songs, Harry Lauder said how pleased he was to be there just to break the monotony. He continued,

'I know that you are wearying and getting anxious to do your part and do your bit but, don't worry, you'll get there. I tell you we are in a great struggle and the man who does not do his duty today will certainly, if he is spared, live to regret it.'

On Saturday 2 October, over 10,000 men took part in a route march through Glasgow. It was felt that by showing off the men in the third line of territorial units that more men would be encouraged to sign up. The troops assembled at Kelvingrove and were ready to move off at 2.10pm. A further 1,700 troops joined them from outside Glasgow with the largest contingents, of 500 men each, representing the Royal Scots Fusiliers, the 4th Cameronians and the 19th Highland Light Infantry together with their pipe bands. The other outside units represented included the 3rd Royal Scots, the 3rd Scottish Borderers, the 3rd HLI, with pipe band, and the 3rd Argyll and Sutherland Highlanders.

On arriving in the city, the extra men were served dinner at St

Andrew's Hall before marching to Kelvingrove Park to join the general units. The route, under the command of Colonel Stanley Paterson, covered many of the main streets of the city and ended up at Glasgow Green.

The Daily Record of Tuesday 5 October reported the arrival of wounded in Glasgow:

> 'Another party of wounded soldiers, fresh from the fighting in France, arrived at the Central Station, Glasgow, last night from the south. They numbered 100, of whom fifty-five were able to walk, the remainder requiring to be borne on stretchers.
>
> The Red Cross and St Andrew's Ambulance wagons conveyed the wounded to Oakbank Hospital, their transfer from the train being carried out by Voluntary Aid Detachments. At the hospital, a party of the RAMC undertook the transfer from the wagons to the hospital beds.
>
> The great majority of the wounded were men of Scottish regiments.'

Rent strikes took hold in the city as landlords raised the payment required for accommodation. *The Manchester Courier* and *Lancashire General Advertiser* of Monday 18 October reported:

> 'In anticipation of attempts to put in force eviction warrants against householders in the Partick district of Glasgow who have refused to pay the increased rents demanded by landlords, a large crowd assembled in the neighbourhood on Saturday. It was soon learned,

Partick rent-strikers' picket at tea. *The Daily Record* **of 22 October stated: These ladies have taken their stand on a commanding situation in Thornwood Avenue, against some of whose householders ejectment warrants have been granted, and no-one is allowed to pass without giving a satisfactory explanation of their business. They possess a bell to inform the neighbourhood of the arrival of the Sheriff's officers.**

A group of nurses at the opening of Bellahouston Hospital on Thursday 14 October. Small girls sold postcards to raise funds.

however, that the property owners had decided not to enforce the orders, owing to the Secretary for Scotland's request to them to hold their hands while the committee which he is appointing makes inquiries into the matter.

Meetings were held at which determination was expressed against allowing families to be ejected and resolutions were passed calling upon the landlords to take off the increases put upon the rents and to refrain from taking any action pending the result of the Government inquiry.

A telegram was read from the Secretary of Munitions stating that his department had no power to interfere in the matter.'

On Thursday 21 October, Michael Gunnan was sentenced to twenty days' imprisonment for assaulting his wife in their house at Adelphi Street in Glasgow.

A plea of insanity was accepted at Glasgow High Court on Tuesday 26 October in a case brought against Elizabeth Murray of 44 Vennel, Greenock. Murray was charged with murdering her husband, Michael, on 11 September.

Helen Boyd, the mother of the accused, said that her daughter and her husband never got on well. She stated that he was very lazy and lost many good jobs through sleeping-in in the morning. Her son-in-law constantly beat her daughter by kicking and butting her.

After many attacks, the accused cut her husband's throat with a razor before fleeing from the house. She then rushed into the Greenock Central

On Saturday 23 October, a fleet of motor ambulances mustered in Blythswood Square, Glasgow and paraded through the streets as part of Red Cross Flag Day. The photo shows one of the ambulances together with a group of Voluntary Aid Detachment nurses.

Police Office saying, 'Keep me, keep me, I have cut my husband's throat with a razor.'

Dr W. Stewart Cook testified that the accused was suffering from temporary homicidal mania and wasn't responsible for her actions at the time.

Lord Guthrie asked the jury to find that the accused has committed the act but was temporarily insane at the time. He explained that she would be acquitted of insanity but would not be liberated. She was ordered to be detained at His Majesty's pleasure.

The City of Glasgow Soldiers' and Sailors' Fund amounted to over £48,000 at the beginning of November. Lord Provost Dunlop expressed the hope that the fund would continue to receive support from the generous and patriotic people of the city.

On Thursday 21 October, the people of Glasgow prayed at St Andrew's Cathedral for the many men lost in battle.

Entertainment in the city continued and in *The Daily Record* of Thursday 11 November there was a report about the reopening of Hengler's Circus. It read:

'With a programme that, it may confidently be stated, will prove as interesting as the best of former years, Mr Hengler's Glasgow Circus reopens on Saturday November 20.

Enlistment proceeded briskly in October at the recruiting offices with Glasgow. The photo shows the medical officer, Captain Fyffe, examining a new recruit at 139 Bath Street. Also shown is Captain Ross, the chief recruiting officer in Glasgow.

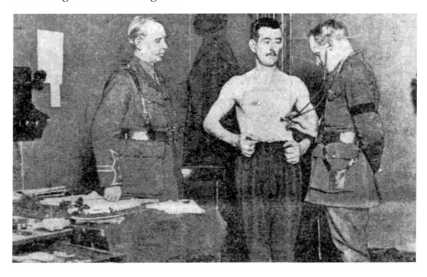

Two men being approached in the Bridgeton district in the hope that they will enlist.

The entertainment will be as diversified as ever, and the great feature again will be a water spectacle, on this occasion entitled 'Silver Falls,' which will be presented in five scenes, each of which will be brimful of thrilling incidents. About forty artistes will be engaged in the performance. Doodles, the popular clown, will again be in the arena with his assistant, August, while the four Italian acrobats and musicians, Gerbolas, who created a great impression in the city four years ago, will also appear. The other artistes on the programme will include Miss Lily, equestrienne; Bros. Freeman, hurricane riders; Duncan's Scotch Collies; The Shannon Family, in an acrobatic and comedy equestrian act; and there will be a sensational performance by three young ladies, three horses and three gigantic elephants.'

On Friday 26 November, four guns which had been captured from the Germans arrived in Glasgow where they were put on show in George Square. They were to remain there for a week before being exhibited in Aberdeen.

At the end of November, a hearing took place involving representatives of the Scottish Union of Dock Labourers, ship owners and stevedores and a demand was put forward for an extra 1d an hour for

Canvassers preparing to take to the streets of Glasgow in November as part of Lord Derby's recruitment scheme. The scheme called on all young single men to enlist in the army.

On Thursday 11 November, the famous American boxer, Jack Johnson, after whom the German 15cm shell was nicknamed, visited the wounded soldiers at Stobhill Hospital. He was accompanied by Mr Morris, his manager. They are shown in the photo with some of the wounded men as well as a group of boy scouts.

men working on the river, with an extra payment for any involved in 'dirty' work.

The Daily Record in December carried the story of the award of the Victoria Cross to Acting Company Sergeant Major James Lennox Dawson who had formerly been a Govan teacher. The story read:

'For most conspicuous bravery and devotion to duty on 13th

A renewed spell of frost in the city on Wednesday 24 November meant that many people took to the ponds to ice skate. The photograph was taken on the Glasgow Skating Club's pond in Great Western Road.

The boxer, Jack Johnson, addressing a meeting in Royal Exchange Square on Thursday 11 November. At least 4,000 people turned up to see the fighter and traffic to Queen Street had to be stopped.

October, 1915, at Hohenzollern Redoubt. During a gas attack, when the trenches were full of men, he walked backwards and forwards along the parados, fully exposed to a very heavy fire, in order to be the one able to give directions to his own sappers and to clear the infantry out of the sections of the trench that were full of gas.

Finding three leaking gas cylinders, he hurled them some 16 yards away from the trench, again under very heavy fire, and then fired rifle bullets into them to let the gas escape. There is no doubt

Argyll and Sutherland Highlanders assisting with Derby recruiting at the Glasgow School Board Buildings in Bath Street on Monday 13 December. Several men interested in enlisting can be seen in the picture.

that the cool gallantry of Corpl. Dawson on this occasion saved many men from being gassed.'

Corporal Dawson, who had formerly been the science master at Hill's Trust School, Govan, later visited his old school and was presented with a gift of a silver tea-service from the pupils and teachers in recognition of his winning the Victoria Cross.

A magistrate and ten councillors were suspended at a meeting of the Glasgow Corporation for refusing to obey the ruling of the chair. The trouble arose because of a refusal to let a demonstration of protest against conscription be held at St Andrew's Hall.

During December, Mr Lloyd George, the minister of munitions, made an inspection of the Clyde munitions area and later held a conference with a number of prominent trade union officials at the Central Station Hotel in Glasgow. This was followed by a tour of various works and factories in the area.

The Daily Record of Saturday 25 December reported on Christmas in the city:

Bugler Hugh Kerr, of the 13th Cameronians, was presented with a gold medal and a special purse of £2 for making the greatest improvement in his physical fitness as part of a class for rejected men. Mr James Dalrymple, of the Glasgow tramways, presented the award at Coplawhill Depot on the evening of Monday 20 December.

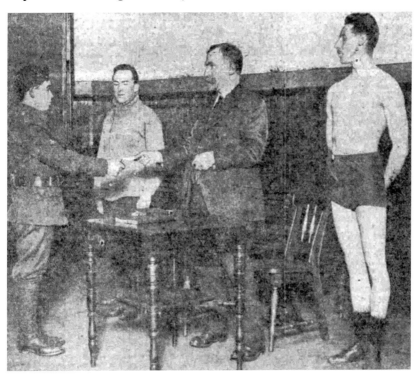

'Practically all the public offices in Glasgow are closed and the holiday feeling was very noticeable in the city last evening. Although the weather broke down and rain fell from seven o'clock onwards, the city streets were thronged.

How plentiful money is was evident in the briskness of shopping. Several shopkeepers remarked that the people were not taking prices into consideration this year. They were procuring the articles they fancied most.

With the curtailment of the train services, together with the demands made on the railways by the war, passenger traffic at the railway termini was little above the normal. Very few people left the city, while the trains from the south had very small complements of visitors.

Where the bustle and stir of Christmastide was most observable was at the post office. Never before had the parcels traffic been so heavy. All day there was a constant stream of people depositing parcels but in the evening, especially, the post office officials were literally besieged. To the war is attributed the enormous increase in parcels as most of them were to soldiers home and abroad. The mail staff of the post office has been considerably depleted since the war began and practically all the sorting is being done by women, while women are also assisting in the work of delivery.

In most of the city chapels, the usual watch-night services were held.

Matinee performances will be given in most instances at the theatres and music halls today and the advance bookings are already stated to be very heavy. Several of the picture houses are opening at an earlier hour and crowded houses are anticipated throughout the day.'

The Daily Record of Wednesday 29 December reported that Lieutenant D. Stanley Dickson, of the 15th Highland Light Infantry, had sustained serious injuries caused by a bursting shell while he was in a dug-out. He was said to have suffered an ugly flesh wound to the ear and severe contusions to the ribs. Lieutenant Dickson was a partner in the firm of Messrs Andersons & Pattison, writers, of Vincent Street, Glasgow.

When war broke out, he joined, through the university contingent, the 6th Cameron Highlanders as a private. Several months later, he was given a commission in the 15th (Glasgow Tramways Battalion) Highland Light Infantry.

Chapter Three

1916 – The Realization

At the Glasgow Coliseum, the New Year's pantomime, 'Jack and Jill', continued to play twice nightly. It was described as 'ideal holiday fare' and featured 'catchy songs, witty comedians, pretty girls, dainty dances and an all star company'.

On Friday 7 January a new depot for making surgical dressings for the wounded was opened. The depot at St John's Road, Pollokshields, Glasgow, was staffed entirely by women volunteers. The premises were opened by Lady Stirling Maxwell. Mrs Herbert, the treasurer, said that, so far, they had received £586 8s 6d in donations.

The Daily Record of Saturday 8 January reported:

'The usual New Year's treat for the wives and children of the soldiers in Glasgow Garrison was given in the Soldiers' Home, Gairbraid Street, Maryhill. Between 300 and 400 sat down to tea and an excellent musical and cinematograph entertainment was afterwards carried through. Amongst those present was Mrs Dunlop (wife of the Lord Provost), Miss Davidson, the lady superintendent of the home, Lieutenant Colonel Radcliffe and several others of the RFA.'

On Saturday 15 January *The Daily Record* reported the death of Sergeant John L. Armstrong of the 16th Highland Light Infantry. He was 33 years old when he died and was the son of the owners of Armstrong's Temperance Hotels in Glasgow. On the day he died, snipers were active and one bullet ricocheted and hit Sergeant Armstrong in the groin. He was given first-aid and removed to the clearing hospital but died shortly afterwards.

On Wednesday 26 January, a fine of £10, with an alternative of twenty-one days

POPULAR AMUSEMENTS.

HENGLER'S

2 PERFORMANCES TO-DAY: 2.30 AND 7.30.

ANNUAL WINTER

CIRCUS SEASON.

BRILLIANT PROGRAMME OF

CIRCUS NOVELTIES.

Including Mr. HENGLER'S NEW WATER SPECTACLE.

"SILVER FALLS"

MATINEES

NEXT WEEK—

MON., WED. AND SAT. AT 2.30 AND EVERY EVENING AT 7.30

Hengler's Circus appeared in Glasgow throughout January and attracted huge crowds. As well as equestrian and animal performances, one of the main attractions was a water spectacle called 'Silver Falls' which showed life as it was in the Wild West.

On 21 January nurses and wounded soldiers from various military hospitals around the city were entertained by the pantomime 'Dick Whittington' at the Coliseum Theatre in Glasgow. The photo shows Miss Victoria Carmen, who played Dick Whittington, together with some of the soldiers.

imprisonment, was imposed on Alexander Carlo. The accused admitted infringing the Liquor Control Regulations by supplying a glass of whisky in licensed premises at Paisley Road West. Matthew McCluny, who received the after hours drink, was also charged and fined £5.

On Friday 4th February, *The Daily Record* featured two soldiers

An RAMC sergeant, and other wounded soldiers, attending the performance of 'Dick Whittington'.

Private J. Gritt, a native of Glasgow, is seen recovering in hospital at Overcliff, Westcliff-on-sea. He was awarded the DCM for rescuing an officer at Neuve Chapelle who had been buried after a shell burst. His father and four brothers had all been killed at the front.

from Glasgow who had been awarded the Distinguished Conduct Medal. After the capture of two Turkish trenches, there was an urgent call for ammunition, sandbags and water. Private Doull and a companion cleared the way of wounded and dead bodies, under heavy fire, so that communication could be made.

Writing to his wife, who lived at Centre Street in Glasgow, he said that he was very proud of the honour. He wrote: 'All I can say

A Highlander having a quick shave while serving with British forces in the Balkans during February. His rifle and uniform are close to hand, ready for action.

is I only did my duty as a soldier and was surprised at what came out of it. I only hope that I will be long spared to wear it for the sake of the 7th and my noble comrades who have fallen in the fight.'

Private Doull joined the Cameronians in October 1915, prior to which he was a baker at J. & B. Stevenson Ltd.

The other recipient of the DCM was Private Gavin Bryce, of the 1/6th Highland Light Infantry, who joined the regiment in April 1912. His wife lived at Waddell Street, South Side, Glasgow.

On Friday 11 February, *The Daily Record* announced the appointment of a military service tribunal for Glasgow:

'The Town Council of Glasgow met specially yesterday to appoint a local tribunal under the Military Service Act, whose business it will be to deal with claims by single men summoned for service under the new statute.

It was explained at the outset by the Lord Provost that the committee, according to the Act, should number not fewer than five and not more than 25. As the labours in Glasgow would be very considerable, he suggested that the number should be 25. An effort by Mr John Stewart to get a lady member appointed was defeated.'

On 21 February, the Battle of Verdun commenced. It proved to be one of the longest and one of the bloodiest of the war.

On Thursday 24 February, Govan Parish Council agreed that representations should be made to the local Government Board asking that payments to old-age pensioners should be increased on account of the higher cost of living.

The Daily Record of Friday 25 February reported news of the Derby Scheme:

'The period of grace permitted single men of military age to enlist as volunteers under the Derby scheme is drawing to a close, and any young men who have not yet seen their way to be attested had better make up their minds at once and enrol their names at the most convenient recruiting station, for after March 1 they will have no choice in the matter. Even yet they have the privilege of joining the Colours as free men – after that date they will be liable by compulsion under the Military Service Act.'

In March, compulsory enlistment for men between the ages of 18 and 41

On Wednesday 1 March, there was a large gathering of farmers at the National Stallion Show which was held at Scotstoun Show Ground. The photo shows Mr Alex Murdoch, Mr William Brown and Mr Alex Buchanan. Horse breeders from all corners of Scotland attended the meeting which was organised by the Glasgow Agricultural Society.

was introduced for single men and childless widowers. However, essential war workers, clergymen, the physically unfit and approved conscientious objectors were exempt. The upper age was later raised to 51.

The Daily Record of Wednesday 15 March reported:

'In the House of Commons yesterday, the Secretary of Scotland said that the total number of prosecutions in Glasgow during the three months ending 29th February, for selling margarine as butter, was eleven, two of which were for selling margarine as Irish butter. All the prosecutions were successful.'

In April, Glasgow bricklayers asked for an increase of wages by an extra 1d an hour.

On Tuesday 4 April, at a meeting of the Clyde Trustees, it was unanimously decided that the wages of employees should be increased in view of the higher cost of living. The increase amounted to 3s a week.

The chairman, Sir Thomas Mason, said that it was gratifying to the men that they were able to carry on their work without resorting to a strike.

During April, the Glasgow Corporation encouraged men to grow their own vegetables for the war effort by giving them land at Tollcross Park. The allotments proved very popular.

On Wednesday 19 April, a story appeared in the local newspaper about the 'glaring lights' in Glasgow:

'Several prosecutions for contravening the regulations for the darkening of the city were heard in the Glasgow Sheriff Summary Court yesterday.

On Saturday 15 April, a seven-a-side hockey tournament was held by the Scottish Women's Hockey Association to raise funds for the Princess Louise Hospital for Limbless Soldiers and Sailors. The event took place at the Western Hockey Club at Kelvinside in Glasgow.

Over 3,000 ladies sold flags on Glasgow's streets on Saturday 15 April in aid of the Scottish Women's Hospitals in France, Salonika and Corsica. The photo shows Glasgow firemen helping with the collection.

Alexander Ramsay Calder, Viewfield Road, Bishopbriggs, admitted having on the 29th of March, between 8 and 8.15 pm, being more than half an hour after sunset, failed to have a scullery light shaded and reduced and the window screened, with the result that more than a dull, subdued light was visible from the outside, contrary to the Defence of the Realm Act.

Mr. Giles, Depute Fiscal, said this man was warned before the prosecution was brought.

Messrs Rowan and Co's weekly supply of kilts being dispatched from their Argyle Street warehouse to the army. Enough kilts to clothe a regiment were sent out each week.

A group of smiling Glasgow Highlanders at the front taken during May.

Sheriff Lee said these regulations would be absolutely useless and ineffective and merely a cause of inconvenience to the citizens if they were not kept by everybody. These prosecutions were to enforce obedience and if small fines did not do it, larger fines would have to be imposed, and, as respondent perhaps knew, these

On Tuesday 9 May, the reconstructed Glasgow post office in George Square was opened by Mr J.A. Pease MP, the postmaster-general. In the morning, Mr Pease witnessed a special parade of the Post Office Cadet Corps in Waterloo Street.

fines could be enormous and ran up to £100. In this case the penalty would be 15s.

This is the first instance in Glasgow of a householder being fined under the new regulations.

A shopman named James White was also fined 15s, for having, at 8 pm, on 30th March, failed to have an inside light obscured and shaded in his shop at Glasgow Road, Rutherglen.

Five other persons were fined 10s each for failing to have lights on vehicles of which they had charge.'

On Monday 24 April, another hospital train arrived at the Central Station in Glasgow. The ninety-one wounded soldiers were conveyed in ambulance wagons to Merryflatts Hospital. They had come direct from the front line and twenty-five of them were in a serious condition. Only six of the men belonged to Scottish regiments.

A meeting was held on Thursday 11 May at St Andrew's Hall by the National Temperance Council of Scotland. It was suggested that prohibition should be introduced and Professor Denney declared that the majority of people in Scotland supported a ban of the sale of alcohol. Over 2,000 delegates, representing 700 public bodies were present. It was decided unanimously that a national appeal for prohibition should be presented to the government.

At a tribunal on Wednesday 17 May, a firm of city mining engineers asked for exemption for seven members of their staff. Ninety per cent of the firm's work involved colliery and underground surveying work. The chairman of the tribunal said that only men involved wholly with surveying could be exempted under the Act. It was agreed that the army had one of the men and the rest were exempted.

Also on 17 May, the funeral of the world-renowned Gaelic ballad singer, Miss Jessie MacLachlan took place at Cathcart cemetery. Two pipers preceded the cortege on the way to the cemetery playing 'The Flowers of the Forest' followed by 'Lovat's Lament'. The pipers were the celebrated John MacColl and J. McDougall Gillies who were both friends of the deceased.

As the coffin was lowered into the grave, the melancholy strains of MacCrimmon's Lament ('Return I Shall Never') were played. Many floral tributes were laid including one from admirers in Australia.

On 31 May, the Battle of Jutland began, a major naval battle crucial to winning the war.

The funeral of Miss Jessie N. Maclachlan, the famous stage singer, at Cathcart Cemetery on Wednesday 17 May. A large assembly of friends and relatives attended.

A Scottish soldier on furlough in Glasgow is seen taking his child for a walk.

On Friday 2 June, *The Daily Record* carried a story under the headline LASCAR MISSIONARY'S BREACH OF REGULATIONS. It read:

'Under the Defence of the Realm Act, an unusual case came before Sheriff Fyfe in the County Buildings, Glasgow, yesterday.

An elderly Indian missionary, named Aziz Ahmed, admitted having removed from Lanark to Rutherglen without the sanction of the military authorities.

The Procurator-Fiscal, Mr P.F. McKenna, informed his Lordship that the accused, who conducted a mission to the Lascars in the city, had been found preaching sedition to the Indian seamen and the military authorities ordered him out of Glasgow, which was a prohibited area. He chose to reside in Lanark, from which place he removed to Rutherglen without permission.

On behalf of the respondent, an agent stated that he had been 39 years in Glasgow. He repudiated the suggestion that he had been abusing his position as a missionary by spreading sedition amongst the Lascars. The missionary pamphlets announced 'Loyalty, peace, goodwill and fraternity'.

His Lordship remarked that he was not concerned with the nature of respondent's mission in Glasgow; it might be a most estimable object, or it might not. What he was concerned with was, that in the opinion of the competent military authorities of the district, it was not desirable that respondent should reside in Glasgow or near it. A fine of £10 was imposed.'

On Saturday 3 June, Lifeboat Day was held in Glasgow. Flags were sold in the streets to raise funds. The city was divided in twenty-two districts and a lady convener presided over each. An army of 2,600 ladies acted as saleswomen. The Flag Day was organised by Mr William Martin, the district secretary for Scotland and the weather for the day, on the whole, was favourable.

On Monday 26 June, whales were spotted in the Clyde and the story was reported in the local paper:

'The crews of the Girvan and district fishing fleets, while prosecuting the herring fishing off the local coast on Monday night, encountered a number of whales and some of these wrought considerable havoc to the herring nets. As many as four whales were seen together and one boat, sailing at full speed, rammed one of the largest.

Two old men, Andrew McQueen and John Ingram, forming the crew of a small sailing boat, had an exciting experience. One of the whales became entangled in the nets of the boat, which was

The Daily Record of Wednesday 31 May noted : 'A Lenzie gentleman is taking a number of wounded soldiers resident in Stobhill Hospital for a trip in his motor car on Sunday afternoons. This photo was taken at the gentleman's home the other Sunday.'

unable to make headway, and ultimately had to be towed to the harbour by a motor boat.

The whale was dead when hauled up onto the beach, where it was found to measure about 30 feet in length and 16 feet in girth. The tail alone was about 7 feet from tip to tip and the fish would weigh several tons.'

The Daily Record of Wednesday 28 June reported that a boy, whose identity had not been established, had been run down and killed by a passenger train at Greenock.

Subscriptions received by Lord Provost Dunlop, of Glasgow, towards the Princess Louise Scottish Hospital for Limbless Sailors and Soldiers at Erskine totalled £93,726 at the end of June.

On 1 July, the Battle of the Somme began. The British Expeditionary Force suffered almost 60,000 casualties on the first day, with 19,240 men killed, making it the bloodiest day in the history of the British Army.

As the Battle of the Somme raged in Europe, relatives back in Glasgow dreaded a knock on the door, as they had throughout the war, of the telegram boy bringing news of their loved ones' death. Newspapers carried the news of all wounded and killed soldiers.

At the beginning of July, amongst the many names of officers reported killed, was that of Second Lieutenant J.N. Carpenter of the Highland Light Infantry. He had recently been awarded the Military Cross for leading a raid into enemy trenches. Before enlisting, he was educated at Glasgow Academy and Glasgow University before joining Messrs Yarrow's shipbuilding yard as an apprentice engineer. He was well known in athletic circles for playing for the Glasgow Academy Rugby Football Club. He joined the army in September 1914.

On Saturday 22 July, a fully equipped ambulance was presented to the Scottish Branch of the Red Cross Society by the Scottish Colliery, Engine and Boilermen's Association. The presentation took place in Blythswood Square, Glasgow.

Sir George Beatson, who accepted the ambulance on behalf of the Red Cross Society described it as a handsome and useful gift. He said: 'We are fighting against a nation of scientific criminals who have devised means of transport hitherto undreamt of. Every motor ambulance given to the Red Cross may be the means of saving men's lives and thus reserving them to help us in the industrial competition

On Wednesday 2 August, a group of 400 wounded soldiers, from various hospitals around Glasgow, were taken on the *Fusilier* for a trip down the Clyde. The photo shows them setting off from Broomielaw.

which will follow the war.'

During July, Councillor James Barrie of Glasgow received news that his son, Lieutenant James Barrie of the Highland Light Infantry, had been wounded in battle and was recovering in a French hospital. Lieutenant Barrie joined the army early in 1915 as a private and soon received a commission. He had been in France since the beginning of 1916.

In August, Margaret Scott McGregor, aged 13, of 15 Hampden Street,

Another shot of a group of wounded soldiers enjoying a day out on the steamer *Fusilier* on Wednesday 2 August. The trip was arranged by Mr T.B. Dunn and friends.

Glasgow, was digging into the bank of the River Blane at Blanefield when she was buried by a fall of earth. After much effort to save her, she was found to be dead.

At the same time, while making his way along the wharf at Prince's Dock, Glasgow, William Hislop, a private watchman, aged 70, fell into the water and drowned.

The Daily Record of Wednesday 30 August carried a story under the headline IMPERSONATION CHARGE : YOUNG MAN ATTEMPTS TO AVOID MILITARY SERVICE. The article read:

'In the County Buildings, Glasgow, yesterday, a peculiar case under the Military Service Act was heard. A youth named William John Carmichael was charged with having (1) on August 19th, represented to a police constable that he was the person to whom a certificate of permanent unfitness for military services had been granted, whereas the certificate did not apply to the respondent, but to another man unknown, whom the accused had induced to personate him; and (2) with being an absentee under the Military Service Act.

Following a plea of guilty, the Fiscal, Mr MacKenna, said the case was a serious one. It came to this that the accused had been called up to military services in March. He got another man who he knew to be permanently unfit to personate him at the Recruiting Office and to appear before the Medical Board. In that way, Carmichael got the notice calling him up endorsed with a certificate of unfitness. As to the charge of being an absentee, it was exceedingly difficult for the military authorities to detect such cases and, as it was believed that such cases of personification were occurring with considerable frequency, he hoped a severe sentence would be imposed.

His Lordship passed sentence of 40 days' imprisonment on the first charge and a fine of 40s on the second – the fine to be deducted from Carmichael's military pay.'

During September, it was announced that Lord Provost Dunlop of Glasgow had received subscriptions totalling £133,614 on behalf of the Scottish Hospital for Limbless Sailors and Soldiers.

The Daily Record of Friday 22 September carried a story concerning the corporation granting a bonus to both male and female tramway employees:

'Wearing the familiar green uniform of the service, employees of the Tramways Department, women and men, were present in strength at the meeting of Glasgow Corporation yesterday. From their place in the public gallery, they followed with interest the discussion respecting wages and war bonus introduced by Mr Montgomery. A tendency displayed at one part by the visitors to take sides in the debate brought the disapproval of members and a reproof from the chairman, Bailie McClure, who, amid cries of "Clear the gallery", explained for the benefit of those who had committed the indiscretion that they were present by courtesy, and therefore must not make demonstrations.

At the end of more than an hour's discussion, in the course of which numerous motions and amendments were offered for acceptance, it was decided that the working week be generally for the period of the war 54 hours, instead of 51 hours, and that time and a half wages be given for the extra three hours.

The question of bonus led to a similar controversy. Finally, it was agreed by the casting vote of the chairman to award weekly 2s to the men and 1s to the women.

An endeavour was made by Mr Dollan to make the concessions retrospective by July 1, but he failed to secure the suspension of the Standing Orders for this purpose.'

Towards the end of September, William McKinnon, aged 66, died from injuries received while trying to board a train at College Station, Glasgow. He was a labourer and resided at 117 Rose Street, Glasgow.

On Saturday 30 September, *The Daily Record* featured a story under the headline GIRLS ON STRIKE. It read:

'Twenty-one girls employed in a brick works in the West of Scotland pleaded guilty at a General Munitions Tribunal in the County Buildings, Glasgow yesterday, to participating in a strike. It was stated that they left work on Monday last and were still on strike. The dispute was one concerning wages.

Sheriff Craigie KC, who presided, asked Miss Young of the National Federation of Women Workers, who acted as an assessor at the Tribunal, if she would endeavour to induce the girls to resume work. Miss Young said she would, and conferred with the girls at the back of the Court.

Mr. J.T. Macfarlane, on behalf of the Ministry of Munitions, and Mr. T.F. Wilson, Clerk of the Court, advised the strikers to return to work. Later the twenty-one strikers returned to the bar of the Court and one of them informed his Lordship that they had decided to resume work immediately.

Sheriff Craigie thanked Miss Young for having given the girls the sound advice to return to work. If the girls had not promised to do so he would certainly have inflicted a heavy penalty. A modified fine of 7s 6d was imposed on each.'

On Monday 9 October, several cases came before the Lanarkshire Military Appeal Tribunal in the County Buildings, Glasgow.

A conscientious objector stated that for the past five years he had been a member of the International Bible Study Association. Opening a bible, he quoted passages which mentioned loving one's enemies. Sheriff Gardner Millar said: 'It is not a case of loving or hating one's enemies. The men going to fight the Germans do not hate them. They fight out of loyalty to their own nation – a totally different thing. Do you suggest that every man in khaki is going out to France out of hate?' The conscientious objector replied: 'No, but God knows no patriotism.' He added that he was against taking up arms against anyone. The tribunal granted exemption from combatant service and a request by the objector to do work of national importance instead was denied by Sheriff Millar.

A tramway motorman claimed exemption at the same hearing, on the grounds that he was a member of the Church of God and could not take up arms. Sheriff Millar asked if the church was recognised in Glasgow and the appellant said that it was and that they met in Burgher Street, Parkhead. However, no minister was attached to the church and anyone could take the service. After discussion, the appeal was dismissed.

The sole proprietor of a second-hand clothes business applied for exemption on account of business hardship, stating that if he had to go to the Army, it would mean serious financial loss. The appeal was dismissed and the military authorities were asked not to call him up until the end of November.

The Daily Record of Tuesday 10 October carried a story under the headline SOLDIER'S LOST SPEECH – REMARKABLE RECOVERY AT A GREENOCK HOSPITAL. It read:

'A curious case of speech recovery has taken place at Smithston War Hospital, Greenock. The consignment of wounded who arrived last week included a Manchester lad, Thomas Shaw, who had lost his power of speech through shell shock. It appears that a gramophone was being used when a record was dropped on a floor. To the surprise of his comrades, Shaw gave a sudden cry of alarm at the mishap, then, realising what had happened, shouted: "Oh, it's come back!" The young soldier belongs to a London regiment.'

An army deserter was jailed on Friday 20 October. The story was featured in *The Daily Record* and read:

'In Glasgow Sheriff Court, a young man named John Brannan was charged before Sheriff Fyfe with having (1) altered and tampered with a military discharge certificate by adding one year to the period of service and making it 1916 instead of 1915, and (2) represented on two occasions that he was the man to whom the certificate applied.

The Fiscal, Mr. P.F. McKenna, said the prisoner applied for work at a munition establishment and would not have been employed had he not been able to show some kind of exemption from the Army. The certificate which he produced applied to another man. The prisoner was a deserter from the Inniskilling Fusiliers. The practice of tampering with certificates was becoming very prevalent.

A Sentence of six months imprisonment was passed.'

A report in a letter to *The Daily Record* told how a battalion of the Argyll and Sutherland Highlanders celebrated Halloween in the trenches. The Regimental Sergeant Major presided at the supper and later there were ample supplies of hazel nuts, roasted chestnuts and apples. Great fun was had as the men tried 'dookin' for apples in a tub of water. One apple contained a lucky silver coin and half a dozen men competed at a time to secure it. After the merriment, a concert followed.

On Thursday 9 November, Sheriff Blair regretted that two hooligans couldn't be flogged. The story was carried in *The Daily Record* and read:

'William Clark and John Murphy, two boys, platers' helpers, appeared before Sheriff Blair at Paisley, yesterday, charged with having, on 2nd inst., in a passenger station at Scotstoun West, and on Yoker Road, assaulted Charles Barbour, an office boy, by jumping on him, attempting to throw him down, kicking him on the legs, and stabbing him on the head, underlip and right hand.

The Fiscal said the lads followed a gang of 16 to 20 shipyard workers who called themselves "The Redskins". On the day mentioned in the charge, they left their work without excuse, and meeting the office boy tried to get him into a row. After assaulting him, they ran away. The cut in the hand had to be stitched and a small artery was severed. Both boys belonged to Bridgeton, Glasgow.

Sheriff Blair described the lads as a pair of miserable little cowards – a couple of young hooligans who were going the way of "The Redskins" gang. There was only one way to deal with that gang. He was sorry Sheriffs had not the power to flog them. Such prisoners were a pest to society and each would receive twelve strokes of the birch – the maximum sentence.'

James Wordie, a member of Shackleton's expedition to the Antarctic, arrived in Glasgow in the early part of November. The explorers had set off in their ship *Endurance* in 1914 but had become trapped in ice in early 1915. The ship eventually sank but all crew members had already left it to live on floating ice. All men survived and were eventually rescued with the last of the men being saved in August 1916.

During the second week of November, Miss Mabel Russell, who was taking a leading part in Harry Lauder's revue, appeared in a playlet called 'Squibs' at the Pavilion in Renfield Street.

On Tuesday 21 November French women munition workers, who were visiting the Clyde district, had the opportunity to inspect local factories. In the afternoon, they were invited to the McLellan Galleries where they saw exhibits and photographs of the work being carried out by British women supplying munitions for the war. Afterwards, they were invited to tea at the City Chambers by invitation of Lord Provost Dunlop.

The Lord Provost said in a short speech that he hoped that the French female munition workers would be able to tell the women of their own country 'how much in earnest the women of Britain were in their work of munition making'. He hoped that it wouldn't be too long before the power of the shells manufactured helped the Allies achieve a glorious victory. There was much applause.

During the middle of December, the pantomime season began in the city. 'Sinbad the Sailor' opened at the Theatre Royal on Saturday 16 December to a huge audience. The show included lavish scenery, dresses and stage effects.

The Daily Record reported:

'There are twelve scenes, the majority of which, depicting the dazzling splendour of the East, are from the clever and imaginative brush of Mr T.F. Dunn. On the rise of the curtain, one views the port of Balsora, a charming and realistic picture, from where

Two hundred wounded soldiers, from hospitals around Glasgow, were invited by the manager of a Sauchiehall Street cinema on Wednesday 8 November to see a film entitled 'The King's visit to his Armies at the Front'.

A wounded soldier having a flag pinned on him during Scotland's Red Cross Flag Day on Saturday 4 November. Although the weather wasn't very good on the day, there was much enthusiasm from the lady flag sellers who collected in thirty-seven districts of Glasgow.

Sinbad sets forth upon his adventures. Later scenes include a shipwreck and The Valley of Diamonds, with which the first act concludes. This is perhaps the most splendid piece of staging in the pantomime.

At the head of the cast is the world-famous Little Tich, who is a host in himself. His inimitable antics, his unique, grotesque, and yet always neat and finished dancing, and his clever songs and patter, are an incalculable asset to the general merriment. He is an artist, "When I was a boy" and "This World's in a Terrible State" are two of his best solo numbers and he introduces his irresistibly humorous scene The Tax Collector.

Miss Ivey Latimer, already an established pantomime favourite in Glasgow, is a charming Principal Boy.

The war, as is natural, is referred to frequently in the gags, as well as in the songs, as when the Old Man of the Sea is interrogated as to whether his group is called up.

The pantomime had an enthusiastic reception from a crowded house, and a successful season, which it certainly deserves, can confidently be predicted.'

On the lead up to Christmas, many generous gifts of game for the wounded were donated to the Red Cross Depot at West Nile Street, Glasgow. In *The Daily Record* of Monday 18 December, it was stated that the game was insufficient to supply all the hospitals in the area and an appeal for more donations of both game and turkey, as well as other gifts, was issued.

Every Gourock soldier and sailor, of which there was over 600 in number, was sent a Christmas parcel from a fund raised by the townspeople. On Monday 25 December, the Belgian refugees in Glasgow were the guests of the Corporation's Belgian Committee in St Andrew's Halls during the evening. The Belgian children, of whom it was estimated that there were well over 1,200 in Glasgow, were also entertained in St Andrew's Halls earlier in the day.

Also, on Christmas Day, local businessmen gave Christmas dinner to the poor of the city. Some 2,500 guests turned up at the forty-seventh annual dinner at the City Hall and partook of customary fare including steak pie and plum pudding.

The Lord Provost congratulated the company on their happy appearance. He said that a great general had said that people who were happy at the present time were a great asset to the nation. Sir Thomas Dunlop asked if those present were downhearted and there was a loud response of 'No!'

Sir Thomas said that that was in the forefront of everything and even on Christmas Day when it was miserable and damp outside, all in the hall were happy. Sir William Robertson told them that 'they should keep their peckers up' and the war will finish sooner.

The Daily Record of Thursday 28 December carried an odd story about an army deserter who had posed as a doctor. The article read:

'Remarkable statements respecting the career of a criminal, David Robson, were disclosed at a sitting of the High Court of Justiciary in Glasgow yesterday. Robson was charged with theft by housebreaking and with being an habitual criminal. He admitted the first part of the charge but denied the second.

A detective described Robson as a dangerous criminal and explained that he was an expert at climbing up rhones [downpipes] to the roofs of dwelling houses. He went through the skylight windows, bored holes in the ceilings of houses, usually above beds, on to which he dropped. Lately, he had taken to breaking into houses and extracting money from automatic gas meters.

Other witnesses stated that he was in the Army, and a corporal from the Scottish Borderers said that he was marked as a deserter from the 2nd September. On 14th September, he took lodgings at Bridgeton and told his landlady that he was a surgical doctor and had just returned after serving two years in France. He called himself "Dr. D. Hamill". To another detective he said he was an American and that his father was allowing him £20 a month.

When he was being questioned in the Western Police Office, he bolted but was subsequently arrested. He then admitted that he was an ex-convict.

Without leaving the box, the jury found the prisoner guilty, and in passing sentence of five years' penal servitude, and seven years' preventative detention, Lord Mackenzie remarked that Robson was a criminal of a dangerous type.'

Chapter Four

1917 – Seeing it Through

On Monday 1 January, Shaw, Walker and Co, based in Union Street, announced that their toy bazaar was now open. They offered a 'larger variety than ever' with 'toys of every description for boys and girls'. Amongst the toys listed in their advertisement were 'a splendid selection of toy soldiers' together with forts, tents and canons.

New Year's Day saw the troops at Maryhill Barracks granted a half-holiday with most of the usual routine drills and parades being dispensed with. A large number of men who came from south of the border were granted special leave over Christmas and the same privilege was granted to Scotsmen over the New Year.

At the beginning of January, the Lord Provost of Glasgow, Sir Thomas Dunlop, sent a telegram to Sir Douglas Haig. It read: 'Glasgow greatly delighted at your promotion to Field Marshal. Heartiest

Scottish pipers at the Battle of the Somme as pictured in *The Daily Record* of Tuesday 2 January. The music was said to spur men on when they were marching or had to go over the top.

congratulations and best wishes for the future of yourself and your noble Army.'

During January, John McNab, a Glasgow youth, was arrested at Islay and charged with deserting from an Admiralty transport at a Clyde port. He was fined £2 with an alternative of 14 days' imprisonment.

In *The Daily Record* of Monday 22 January, it was reported that Captain John Warnock, of the Royal Engineers, had been awarded the Military Cross. Before enlisting, he had worked for Messrs Formans and McCall of Glasgow.

The death of a miner in a traffic accident was reported in the newspaper under the headline DARK STREET PERILS in late January:

'In attempting to cross Pollockshaws Road, Glasgow, on Saturday evening, Charles Gould (44), 27 Strathclyde Street, was killed. Two motor lorries were passing at the time, one having the second, which had broken down, in tow. It is conjectured that the unfortunate man did not observe the second vehicle. Death was due to fracture of the skull.'

On Thursday 25 January, celebrations were held to mark the anniversary of Robert Burns birth. *The Daily Record* reported:

'While the public celebration of the anniversary of the birth of Robert Burns was less pronounced than formerly because of the war, nature appropriately blew a 'blast of January wind', as if to remind us of the memorable occasion.

The statue in George Square, Glasgow, was tastefully decorated, as is usual, by the local Burns Clubs. The flowers and evergreens were supplied by Lord Rosebery and others, while the pedestal also bore the suitable quotation: "I came to congratulate my country that the blood of her ancient heroes still runs uncontaminated."

Among the few suppers held in honour of the occasion, the most important, so far as Glasgow was concerned, was that of the Scottish Burns Club in the Douglas Hotel, Bath Street.'

On 28 January, *The Sunday Post* announced that Corporal Jack Deans had been awarded the Military Medal. He joined the Business Battalion of the Highland Light Infantry at the opening of hostilities and had been in France since November 1915.

Court action was taken for a breach of promise towards the end of January and the story was carried in *The Daily Record* of Friday 26 January. It read:

> ' "After the way he has disgraced me, I would on no account marry him now," said a young woman of prepossessing appearance, named Agnes Macbrierley, residing at 101 Cotton Street, Castle Douglas, who figured as the pursuer in an action concluding for £250 damages for breach of promise of marriage, held in the County Buildings, Glasgow, yesterday, before Sheriff Thomson.
>
> The defender, who was not present in Court, was William McGarva, tramway motorman of 1011 Duke Street, Glasgow, now in the Army.
>
> The pursuer, replying to her solicitor, Charles McMillan, said she was 21 years of age and first met the defender at Castle Douglas in 1912. She met him again in August 1914, when he was on holiday at Drybridge, Gatehouse. He called at Castle Douglas to see her brother, whom he knew. They went for a walk and, in the course of their talk, the defender asked her if she enjoyed her holidays. She said that she did and he then invited her to spend them in Glasgow. He remarked that she could stay with his half-sister, a married woman with whom he lodged.
>
> She said that she would like to go to Glasgow and the following month, she got a weekend, which she spent there. One of her brothers was at the same time lodging in the house. The defender paid her great attention – in fact, made love to her.
>
> On returning home, she received a letter from him addressed "My dearest Agnes" and a weekly correspondence was carried on between them. In January 1915, at his suggestion, she got a situation at Hyndland, Glasgow, in order to add to their happiness. He walked her out regularly and ultimately said he would marry her as soon as he had sufficient money. Defender had since declined to fulfil that promise.
>
> Defender stated that although he was employed as a motorman by Glasgow Corporation, he had not been exempted from military service. He was an attested man and, having been passed fit, he may be called up at any time and was therefore not in a position to marry pursuer. It was unreasonable, he said, to exact fulfilment of his promise until the conclusion of the war.'

The case was adjourned until further evidence could be submitted.

Wounded soldiers from various hospitals around Glasgow attended a service at Springburn Parish Church Hall on the afternoon of Saturday 17 February. The smiling soldiers can be seen here accompanied by their nurses.

Over 3,000 ladies sold flags in Glasgow on Saturday 17 February to raise funds for the work of the Scottish Churches in France. Although the weather wasn't favourable, the appeal met with an enthusiastic response. Huts were already in operation for the soldiers in France but there was a demand for more and the funds were required for maintenance as well as to expand the scheme.

On Monday 19 February, *The Daily Record* reported a serious fire in the city with an estimated loss of £40,000. The story read:

'Serious was the fire which occurred in one of the most congested areas in the heart of Glasgow yesterday, although it had a redeeming feature; it was free from fatality or accident.

The outbreak took place in a block of buildings bounded by Candleriggs, Wilson Street and Brunswick Street. Its seat of origin was a structure, measuring 100 feet in length, and 40 feet in breadth, rising to a height of four storeys. The premises stand on what is known as Smith's Court and are occupied by Messrs Robert Hamilton & Son Ltd., calenderers.

Several people seemed to become aware of the outbreak simultaneously. In one instance, a man who occupies a house on the top flat at 70 Brunswick Street, with his wife and three daughters, was wakened by the smell of burning material and a loud crackling noise. Scantily attired, the family made a hurried exit to the street. Fears being entertained that the flames, even early in the progress of the outbreak, might spread to a hotel in the neighbourhood, the occupants were roused from slumber and apprised of the risk. At 2.45 a.m. such an intimation was scarcely pleasing.

Called by Constable Turner, the fire brigade were quickly on the scene. Detachments were present from the Central, Southern, Eastern, Western and Springburn stations of the brigade. With many lines of hose in action, they laboured to minimise the loss.'

In February, the Countess of Eglinton formally opened a new creche in connection with the Phoenix Park Kindergarten, Cowcaddens in Glasgow. She said that 'child welfare was one of the most important matters that could be taken up at present – second only to winning the war – and that the care of children was the most valuable asset of the British nation.'

In the middle of February, a new order was introduced by the Food Controller to ensure that the price of potatoes wasn't vastly inflated due to a shortage of supplies.

The Daily Record reported:

'Glasgow dealers are at their wits end on how to solve the potato problem. For weeks it seems that the Order which comes into operation today would press heavily upon them, in view of the shortage of local supplies, which shortages have necessitated the augmenting of stocks from distances as far south as London.

On the market figures, retailers are purchasing at 20s per bag of 12 stones. By the terms of the Order, they will be expected to sell at 1s 9d per stone. In selling by retail, there is always a certain amount of loss. Rather than incur risk, it is considered likely that many may cease to stock potatoes. Thus householders in the West of Scotland may be unable to obtain supplies.'

On Wednesday 21 February, *The Daily Record* carried a story entitled GIRL WORKERS AND THEIR PAY. It read:

'On complaining to their foreman that their wages were inadequate, a dozen girls employed by a box-making firm were ordered out of the factory and got their leaving certificates. Yesterday, they appeared at the Glasgow Munitions Tribunal in support of an application for compensation in lieu of a week's notice.

Replying to Sheriff Fyfe, who presided, one of the girls said a deputation was sent to the manager asking for an increase in wages but it was refused.

It was stated that the manager was not present in court and his Lordship said that was unfortunate as the girls' claim must therefore hold good. A week's wages was granted each of the girls.'

A total of £93 was accumulated at the beginning of March for the

Soldiers' and Sailors' Help Society. The money was raised with the aid of collection boxes on Glasgow tramcars.

On Tuesday 6 March, eight squads of riveters, each comprising twenty-four men, were prosecuted by the Ministry of Munitions in Glasgow for failing to work diligently. The men all pleaded not guilty.

Mr McLachlin, who represented the Ministry of Munitions, said that the men did not complete sufficient work during a certain week stated. The men had been concerned about pay. They had been offered 13s 6d per 100 rivets but declined this offer. After seeing their shop stewards, the price offered was 16s 8d but, again, this was refused by the workers. The work was urgent and the management had no alternative but to pay the riveters 11¾d per hour.

However, when the management visited the job, they found that the work was progressing most unsatisfactorily. They contacted the shop stewards who told the men that they would have to do more but one man commented that they wouldn't do any more than they were doing at the time. The men's wages were increased to 20s 10d per 100 rivets and the job was completed.

One witness stated that some of the squads had men who were ill and others had been engaged in jobs in other parts of the yard so couldn't keep up the quota on the particular job stated. On hearing this, Mr Mackie, presiding, suggested that the case be withdrawn so as to maintain the amicable working arrangements which had already existed in the yard. Mr McLachlin was unhappy with this and the case against the men was withdrawn but it was impressed, in the strongest terms, that no slacking should take place in the future.

On 15 March, Nicholas II, the Russian Tsar, abdicated.

On 24 March, *The Yellowstone News* in Montana carried the headline, U.S. EXPECTED TO ANNOUNCE THAT STATE OF WAR EXISTS. The newspaper went on to report that 'News received from Plymouth that fifteen men, some of them Americans, had been drowned when the American merchantman *Vigilancia* was sunk without warning by a German submarine.' The story also stated that 'President Wilson is expected, within 48 hours, to indicate definitely that he believes a virtual state of war exists between the United States and Germany.'

On Wednesday 28 March, *The Daily Record* reported on a recent court case:

'Three prisoners on remand from Glasgow appeared at the bar of the High Court of Judiciary in Edinburgh for sentence by Lord Salvesen. John McGlin, a despatch clerk, was sent to penal servitude for five years for the theft of £6 7s; Archibald Carter was sent to penal servitude for four years in respect of theft from his employer; and a similar sentence was imposed upon Maria Freedman for committing seven acts of theft from passengers on tramway cars.'

At the beginning of April, John Egan, a soldier, was sent to prison for 14 days at Govan Police Court for assaulting his wife by striking her on the head with a cane.

Joseph Moore, aged 29, a chauffeur, had been missing from his home in Adelphi Street, Glasgow since 2 March. He was later found drowned in the River Clyde early in April.

On 5 April, the *Evening Herald* reported: 'The U.S. Senate has passed the resolution declaring a state of war with Germany by 82 votes to 6 at 11.15pm after 13 hours continuous debate. There was no demonstration when the result was announced.'

Mrs Ronald Gordon, who was attached to the Red Cross Transport Depot, left Aberdeen on Friday 30 March for Glasgow en route to Southampton. She then travelled abroad with her car to assist the Red Cross Work being done there.

America joined the war on 6 April, 1917.

On 10 April, a bring and buy sale was organised by London Road United Free Church in Glasgow and yielded over £90 for the war fund.

The Daily Record of Wednesday 11 April reported on the answer to the dwindling supplies of potatoes in the city. The story read:

'About 100 tons of English potatoes, all of excellent quality, arrived in Glasgow yesterday under the scheme of the Government to relieve the almost total dearth of supplies in Scotland.

This is by far the largest quantity that has come to hand, and is considerably more than the total of the daily supplies which have come dribbling in for the past week.

There is now hope that daily supplies will be forwarded in

sufficient quantities to meet the reasonable requirements of the community until the new crop becomes available at the end of next month or the beginning of June. It will be recalled that 12,000 tons have been earmarked by the Government as Glasgow's pro rata share.'

The Daily Record of Friday 20 April reported:

'After the revolting disclosures of the horrors of the Hun corpse factory and the deliberate sinking of hospital ships – to say nothing of the many other appalling atrocities which the Germans are committing in all directions – it is both suprising and disgusting to hear the Pacifists in Parliament still raising their voices in the interests of the foe, who is slowly but surely approaching defeat.'

Towards the end of April, Peter Logan, aged 9, the son of a miner residing at 890 Great Eastern Road, Glasgow, was knocked down and killed while crossing Great Eastern Road.

Also late in April, the body of a Mrs Gibson was found floating off Gourock Pier. She was a widow who resided at 182 West Princes Street, Glasgow. She had been seen on the pier an hour earlier.

The British Transport *Transylvania* was sunk by a torpedo on 4 May with a loss of 413 lives. Paul Hunter, a fireman on board the ship, from Perth Street in Glasgow, said: 'I was below at the time she was first struck and the explosion burst the main steam-pipe and extinguished the electric lights. We had to find our way as best we could from the stokehold in the darkness. Boats were being lowered away when we got on deck and I noticed, with much satisfaction, that first place was being given to the women who were with us, and that there was an entire absence of excitement on the part of both sailors and soldiers. The captain of the *Transylvania* was at his post and his first words were 'Keep cool'.

They eventually got away safely. One man managed to rescue his white cat while another saved his French poodle.

The Daily Record of Saturday 5 May campaigned against food wasters in the city: 'There is no blinking the fact that a considerable part of the population pay no attention whatever to appeals for economy in the use of food.

Paul Hunter, a survivor from the torpedoed *Transylvania*. Hunter, a fireman from Glasgow, was below deck when the attack took place but managed to get to the deck in the darkness to make it to a lifeboat.

As recorded in another column, a young woman was observed in a Glasgow tearoom yesterday to take eight heaped-up spoonfuls of sugar in her glass of lemon squash. This case, we have reason to believe, is typical. There are hundreds of these placid young ladies who have absolutely failed to realise that there is any reason why they should stint themselves in the slightest degree. They don't read the appeals which appear in the press, whether issued by the King or Food Controller; they pay no attention to leaflets or the eloquence of food economy orators. They simply do not understand that the nation of which they form a part is fighting desperately for its life, and so long as they can get it, they will use sugar wastefully to sweeten their lemon squash and eat cakes and chocolates, whenever they get the opportunity, quite irrespective of actual need. They are not knowingly unpatriotic; they are only thoughtless and unconcerned regarding the course of the grim tragedy of the world war.

Andrew McLay was well-known onboard the *Transylvania* as 'The Diver'. Whenever the liner was in port, he would dive into the water for a swim from a height of 62 feet. His ability as a strong swimmer allowed him to rescue not only his Persian cat, Gaby, but also Second Engineer T. Ross who would have drowned had it not been for McLay's swimming abilities.

People who can't fight and won't work should at least be prevented from wasting the food resources required to keep the nation's workers and fighters in full vigour.

Compulsory rationing may be regarded as undesirable. But if it is to be avoided, the scandal of waste must be ended and to do this, something much more effective than the existing food restricting orders will have to be devised.'

Charles Armstrong, a labourer, severely assaulted two policemen in Centre Street, Glasgow on Saturday 5 May. He appeared before the Southern police court and was sentenced to three months' imprisonment with hard labour. One of the policemen was rendered unfit for duty.

The Daily Record of Friday 25 May reported on the movements of the 'Tank':

'The model Tank constructed by the staff of Cowlairs Locomotive Works and the Springburn Fire Brigade will make two tours in

The Glasgow Tramway prize scheme continued to flourish. The photo shows a man buying a ticket from a conductress on Monday 28 May.

Glasgow tomorrow in connection with the Soldiers' and Sailors' Flag Day. Souvenirs postcards of the 'Tank', priced 2d, will be sold.'

On Saturday 26 May, an article about the care of war orphans appeared in the newspaper and read:

'Glasgow School Board are to open centres where children, left orphans by the death of parents or guardians while serving with the forces, and other scholars deprived of home supervision on account of the absence of parents or guardians at work, may assemble for meals and have facilities for preparing home lessons.'

Towards the end of May, several employees of the railway appeared in court charged with theft:

'Dishonest acts on the part of railway servants led to several men appearing in the dock of Glasgow Sheriff Criminal Court before Sheriff Dods.

William Ralston, engine driver; William Henderson, assistant yardsman; and Archibald McSporran, yardsman, all in the employment of the Caledonian Railway, were charged with a series of thefts from goods trains on various parts of the railway system. Modified pleas of guilty were tendered in each case.

The Fiscal, Mr Strathern, said that particularly from the point of view of the company and of the commercial community, these offences were of a serious nature. The railway companies made great complaint of such offences at the present time on account of their being understaffed and unable to give proper supervision to goods in transit. It was regrettable, too, that trusted servants of the company should stoop to this sort of thing.

His Lordship said that he would take into account the prisoners' long service with the company. He imposed a penalty on each of £25, with the alternative of 60 days imprisonment.

At the same Court, James Hamilton, engine-driver on the Caledonian Railway, admitted the theft of a shirt and four railway uniform jackets from a goods train, while John Morrison, engine-driver, pleaded guilty to resetting a quantity of cakes of soap. In each case the same penalty of £25 was imposed. His Lordship granted time in which to pay the fines.'

Annie McLean, aged 70, of Kelvinhaugh Street, Glasgow died at Western Infirmary at the beginning of June. She had sustained a fracture of the skull after being hit by a tramcar while crossing Argyle Street.

An open-air concert was given in Queen's Park, Glasgow, on Saturday 9 June to raise funds for the Scottish Blinded Soldiers and Sailors Fund. The concert was given by the Govanhill Parish Church Junior Choir. Fine summer weather favoured the occasion and an audience of several thousand gathered around the bandstand.

At previous fetes, the choir had raised a total of £426 for various war schemes and it was the object of Mr John Thomson, the conductor, to raise £50 at this occasion.

Familiar choruses included 'The Farmer's Boy' and 'The Battle of Stirling' along with a rendition of the National Anthem. Mr Thomson sang solos and there were graceful exhibitions of dancing including Highland and Irish sets as well as Morris dances.

Mr James Dalrymple, the general manager of the Glasgow tramways, expressed thanks to all who took part.

During the course of the afternoon, a case of half a dozen silver teaspoons, which had earlier been presented to Mr Thomson, were handed over to the chairman who put them up for auction. They fetched £2 3s 6d which went towards the fund.

On Monday 11 June, a food exhibition was opened at 461 Dumbarton Road, Glasgow. Cooking demonstrations and sample meals were laid out in accordance with the regulations of the Ministry of Food. Sir

The Official Air Services Exhibition was opened in the McLellan Galleries on Monday 25 June by His Grace the Duke of Atholl MVO DSO. Also present at the opening was Lieutenant A.J. Roberts, RNAS, the Countess of Drogheda, Sir Thomas Dunlop and Lady Dunlop.

Samuel Chisholm emphasised how a great part of winning the war was played by those at home whose job it was to economise on food and not let anything go to waste.

The Daily Record of Tuesday 26 June reported on the case of John MacLean, an imprisoned school teacher. The story read:

'Mr Watt asked the Secretary of Scotland, in the House of Commons yesterday, whether he would not consider the advisability of liberating from jail John Maclean, a graduate of Glasgow and a school teacher by profession, who has been imprisoned for more than a year under the Defence of the Realm Act for making speeches of an inflammatory character, in view of the fact that prisoners of other nationalities are being released wholesale by order of the government.

Mr. Munro stated that John MacLean had now served more than half of the normal term for which he would be under detention. He continued: "I have come to the conclusion, having regard to all the circumstances, and in particular to the possible effect of continued imprisonment upon his health, that I am justified in sanctioning his early release on licence; and I propose to issue instructions to that effect."

His comments were met with cheers.'

On Friday 13 July, a bigamy trial was reported in the local newspaper:

'The story of a married man who married a soldier's widow in order to get the £52 Army grant due to her on her re-marriage was told in Glasgow Sheriff Court yesterday, when Peter Derrick (25) and Elizabeth Dennis or O'Connell (21) were charged before Sheriff Scott Moncrieff with bigamy.

The offence was admitted and it was stated that Derrick was a farm servant and that his wife and two children resided at Stevenston. The female prisoner was the widow of a soldier who was killed on service. She also had two children and knew of the existence of Derrick's wife at Stevenston. The couple were married in March last and cohabited together.

An agent for the woman said that it became known to the male prisoner that a soldier's widow was entitled to £52 on re-marriage. It was he and his relatives who induced her to go through a form of marriage so that this money could be got. After the £52 had been obtained, the woman was thrown aside like a dirty rag. The money was taken from her in driblets by Derrick.

His Lordship sentenced Derrick to three months' imprisonment and the woman to one month's imprisonment.'

James Kemp, described as a middle-aged man, appeared before Sheriff Thomson at Glasgow on Thursday 26 July. He admitted to a charge of robbing a man in Milton Street, Cowcaddens, of a watch and chain, a purse and medal and 30s.

The prisoner had been observed going through the pockets of a drunk man by a woman in Milton Street. When she tried to stop him, he threatened to strike her. A crowd gathered and refused to let the prisoner escape.

It was stated that there had only been four years since 1901 that Kemp had not been in prison. He was found guilty and sentenced to 15 months' imprisonment with hard labour.

Toward the end of July, a frame maker appealed for exemption. The story was carried in *The Daily Record*:

'A busy day was again experienced at the Lanarkshire Military

Appeal Tribunals in Glasgow yesterday.

At the Court, over which Mr. T.F. Wilson presided, a man of small stature appealed on conscientious grounds. He described himself as a picture-frame maker but said he was formerly a telegraphist, which occupation he gave up on account of the fact it involved Sunday work. He was a member of the International Bible Society and his conscience was against killing. Each man's conduct, he considered, should be guided by his own conscience. If a man believed he had a right to fight, he should fight.

The Chairman remarked that according to the appellant's statement, that if a man thought he had a right to steal then he should steal. The appeal was refused.'

The Battle of Passchendaele, also known as the Third Battle of Ypres, began on 31 July.

August started off with blue skies and sunny weather and it was reported that many trippers took themselves off to train stations in and around Glasgow to head for the coast. Numbers had greatly increased and the numbers of holidaymakers leaving the city was reminiscent of happier times before the war started.

On Thursday 2 August, the story of a comedian's continued exemption was carried in *The Daily Record*. It read:

'Urging that "Neil Gow", to give respondent his stage name, should take up work of national importance, the military representative at Lanarkshire Tribunal, in Glasgow yesterday, appealed against the continued exemption of the comedian on medical grounds.

After explaining that his client had been rejected on three occasions, and that he was neither a trained clerk nor tradesman, Mr A. Shaughnessy mentioned that "Gow" sang several songs on the lines which Harry Lauder had made familiar, adding, "There is no rough and tumble work."

Laughingly, Sheriff Lee asked what Lauder would say to that. It was stated further by Mr Shaughnessy that "Gow" sang to wounded soldiers.

On the medical certificate being produced, the Tribunal continued the exemption. "Keep on entertaining wounded soldiers," was the advice of the Sheriff.'

On Saturday 18 August, at Glasgow Cathedral, Captain Roy Young MC (RAMC) was married to Miss Elizabeth Hay, a matron at Elderpark Hospital. The photo also shows Sir George Beatson who gave the bride away.

Mary Strafford, a female chauffeur was fined 20s at Dunoon on Friday 17 August for reckless driving which resulted in a Glasgow man being knocked down.

On Saturday 18 August, Sir Robert Baden-Powell visited Glasgow where he inspected a rally in Queen's Park Recreation Ground. Accompanied by Lady Baden-Powell, they were met by between 3,000 and 4,000 boy scouts. As the boys paraded by their Chief Scout, they cheered and waved their hats. Patrols gave displays of first-aid, signalling, knot-tying, cooking and boxing. At the end of the meeting, Baden-Powell thanked the boys for doing their bit for their country and he hoped that they would keep on doing their duty even when the war was over.

Following the rally, Sir Robert was the guest of 400 scoutmasters and patrol leaders in the Grand Hotel, Charing Cross in Glasgow. After tea, there were musical performances which ended with everyone singing enthusiastically 'He's a Jolly Good Fellow'.

Later in August, the Locomotive Engine Drivers' and Firemen's Society persisted in their threat to call a strike unless the president of the Board of Trade agreed to an eight-hour working day. The society was told that an eight-hour working day was unacceptable but the matter would be given consideration once the war was over. A proclamation was issued as part of the Munitions Act stating that the strike would be

Girl harvesters taking a rest among the stooks. Women workers played a vital role during wartime and were essential at harvest time when most male labourers were away fighting in the war.

illegal and that the dispute should be referred to the Ministry of Labour for arbitration.

On Friday 7 September, a free rest and tea room was set up for wounded sailors and soldiers. It was located at 4 Bothwell Street, Glasgow, and was known as 'The Blue Boys' Club'. The club was equipped with tables and comfortable chairs with the provision for playing cards, draughts and dominoes.

Ex-Provost Blakeley explained that the people of Glasgow had felt sorry for wounded men, especially those with no money in their pockets and nowhere to go. He said: 'Some of the citizens decided that the boys in blue should have a place which should be entirely their own and into which they could come every afternoon and have a rest, tea, a game and a look at the papers.'

Mrs Low, the convener of the ladies' committee in charge of the scheme, formally declared the club open. The proceedings terminated with the singing of the National Anthem.

During September, Sergeant Barry, of the Scots Guards, was awarded the Italian Bronze Medal for Military Valour. Before the war, he was a member

The King arriving at Ibrox Park on Tuesday 18 September. The King is seen being driven in an open car around the track as women munition workers cheer him on. The Royal Investiture was the first held in Scotland for over 100 years and the first public ceremony of its kind in Scotland.

Bailie Stewart being made an Officer of the British Empire for his work helping the Belgian refugees in Scotland. He is being awarded the honour by the King at Ibrox Park on Tuesday 18 September.

The King arriving at the City Chambers with Lord Provost Sir Thomas Dunlop on 18 September. The king received an enthusiastic welcome from the crowd and the guard of honour was provided by the City of Glasgow Volunteers.

of the Glasgow Southern Division Police Force.

The Daily Record of 19 September reported on Harry Lauder's appeal at a Glasgow concert:

'Every seat was occupied in St Andrew's Hall, Glasgow, last night, at the concert in aid of the Harry Lauder Million Pound scheme for Scottish sailors and soldiers maimed in the war. Lord Balfour of Burleigh, who presided, explained the object of the fund.

Mr. Lauder sang some of his recent successes and also two new songs entitled, "Private Jock McDade" and "We a' go hame the same way".

At the close of the concert, Mr Lauder made an appeal for the people of Scotland to assist him in the object in view. He said that if we failed to do our duty to the fighting men who returned home broken in the war, it would be a lasting disgrace.

He was out for £1,000,000. They knew that the maimed soldiers would get a pension but that would not be sufficient to enable them to make a fresh start in life. If, after the war, he saw a maimed

On Saturday 22 September, a building belonging to Messrs W. McLaren, Sons & Co was destroyed by fire. The total damage was estimated at £140,000.

soldier standing at a street corner selling laces or matches he (Mr Lauder) would wish to God that their sons had never laid down their lives for their country.

Two thousand wounded sailors and soldiers from the city hospitals were entertained by Mr Lauder at a special matinee in the Glasgow Alhambra yesterday afternoon. Mr Harry Lauder sang four songs.

On Friday 21 September, at Glasgow Northern Police Court, William Drummond Cameron, aged 32 and a draper's salesman, was fined £2 and handed over to the military authorities as an absentee. He had previously claimed that he was a conscientious objector.

During October, Private William Dobie

A popular 'Women, past, present and future' pageant was held in Glasgow on Saturday 22 September on behalf of Scottish Meat and Allied Trades. The float represented the many land workers.

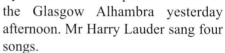

appeared in court charged with murder. The story was carried in *The Daily Record* of Friday 19 October under the headline, VERDICT OF MURDER AGAINST GLASGOW SOLDIER. It read:

'A verdict of wilful murder was returned yesterday against Private William Dobie at an inquest held at Faversham, Norwich, on Helen Dobie, his wife, whose dead body was found lying at the roadside with her throat cut last Monday morning. The husband was not at the inquest.

John Dumbleton, 146 Pollokshaws Road, Glasgow, father of the deceased, said they were married last June. The husband was then engaged in mine-sweeping but in July, he joined the Army. The witness knew little about the husband, who repeatedly requested his wife to join him in Faversham, and she left Glasgow to do so on the 7th inst. Letters arrived in Glasgow for her after that date, in one of which the husband reproached his wife with neglecting to write him though writing to others:

"I have loved you for nearly three years now, and I think your love for me is false, and so I am finished now. Yes, once and for all, so forget me as I have already you. This is the finish now, so don't look at me or write again, as I don't wish you to do so. Never claim me as your husband, your sickened and broken-hearted husband."

Mrs Dobie was only 21 last Sunday.'

During October, a Glasgow motor company was fined £10 for storing 110 gallons of petroleum without first obtaining a licence.

An unusual appeal was made for exemption at the Military Tribunal. The story was carried in *The Daily Record* of Thursday 25 October:

'On the ground that he had signed in July 1914, a declaration that he would not fight against Germany in the event of war against Britain, a single man, described as a warehouseman, appealed for exemption at the Lanarkshire Military Tribunal in Glasgow yesterday.

The appellant stated that he was on holiday in Germany, and before being allowed to leave on July 28 1914, he had to make this promise. The penalty for non-compliance was death. If sent to join the British Army in France, the result would be that, if unfortunate to be captured, he would be shot.

Sheriff Lee, the chairman, said this was not a matter with which the Tribunal could deal. It was a matter to be carefully inquired into and he asked the military representative to make a note of the special circumstances before calling up the appellant.'

At the beginning of November, while crossing Abercromby Street in Glasgow, six-year-old Christina Forsyth, whose father was a prisoner of war in Germany, was knocked down by a tramway car and killed.

On 7 November, the Bolsheviks successfully overthrew the Russian government.

On Tuesday 21 November, Margaret Laing of 660 Dalmarnock Road, Bridgeton was fined £5, with the option of 30 days' imprisonment, for professing to tell fortunes by palmistry.

On Tuesday 27 November, James Sweeney, an Army absentee, was sent to prison, by the Eastern Police Court of Glasgow, for 30 days for assaulting the policeman who arrested him.

On 28 November, it was reported that John Cullen, a carter, was sent to prison for 21 days for stealing 12lbs of margarine from a box that he was conveying to the Central Station in Glasgow.

Towards the end of November an article appeared in *The Daily Record* under the headline GERMANS IN GLASGOW. It read:

'At a meeting in the Merchants' House, Glasgow, yesterday, under the auspices of the British Empire Union, Mr J.E. Blakeborough, organiser of the Union, said he had been sent to Glasgow to find out why so many unnaturalised Germans were still at large in Glasgow and the Clyde district, and his instructions were to forward the names and addresses of such persons to London. The object of the British Empire Union was to keep the British Empire for the British.

Ex-Councillor Whitson moved that they form a branch of the Union in Glasgow. The resolution was seconded by Mr T.R. Ker, Dougalston, who said we were in danger so long as Germans were allowed so much freedom as they enjoyed at present to move about in Glasgow. They might be good Germans; but for ten such there might be one bad German, and one bad German, if loose, may play the devil.

The resolution was adopted and a committee appointed.'

On Friday 30 November, the question of new gaming machines was raised in the city. The story was carried under the headline BAILIE'S BAN ON RETURN-MONEY TYPE. The story read:

'An important decision under the Gaming Machine (Scotland) Act, given yesterday at St Rollox Police Court, Glasgow, affected, it is believed, a large number of new penny-in-the-slot machines in ice cream shops in Glasgow.

An effort was made by the defence to have it declared that a penny-in-the-slot machine, which in the successful manipulation of the balls, returns the penny, was not a machine that constituted a contravention of the Act.

The machine, known as "The Conquerer's Flags", was operated by a police sergeant in court, but without success. A constable stated that he and another three witnesses had tried the machine, and all three had lost their pennies.

For the defence, it was contended that it was a game of skill, and that it was a machine similar in principle to the football and cricket machines at railway stations.

Superintendent Muir held that the machine was built for the purpose of evading the Act, and that it was not a game of skill but a game of sport, hazard or competition. He quoted a recent High Court decision in support of his contention.

Bailie Macnab found the charge proved and imposed a fine of three guineas on the respondent, Richard Jaconelli, 162 Castle Street, Glasgow, and ordered the machine to be forfeited.'

As the result of a two-day carnival held in the St Andrew's Halls in Glasgow, a sum of over £2,600 was raised. The money was to be used to provide hospitals, operating theatres and ambulances for war horses. The carnival was opened by the Honorable Mrs Gideon Murray on Saturday 8 December. She said that 'the function was different from any other, as the horses could not in anyway express gratitude for what was being done for them.' She continued, 'While Glasgow was doing so much for the war horses, there were many horses in the city suffering greatly because of short rations and inexperienced drivers.' She suggested that the society should consider whether it was possible to hold a 'Kindness to Animals Day', at which funds would be collected for the purpose of educating people in the care of horses.

An auction sale was conducted during the day by Mr R.J. Edgar and 'Doodles' from Hengler's Circus.

On 9 December, a large number of discharged soldiers and sailors attended a public meeting of the West of Scotland Sailors' and Soldiers' Federation and Welfare League in the Metropole Theatre in Glasgow.

Mr Donlevy said that the purpose of the meeting was to see that the men and their families, who were affected by fighting in the war, should be treated properly. Twenty thousand cases had already been dealt with

Merryflats War Hospital in December. The ward has been decorated for the Christmas celebrations.

in Edinburgh and many men had secured pensions even after being refused them by the responsible authorities.

The pantomime season got under way in Glasgow on Friday 14 December when 'Dick Whittington' opened at the Alhambra. *The Daily Record* reported:

'Chastity of taste is everywhere apparent, even when the gorgeous and imposing is essayed, and the level of high excellence is maintained marvellously throughout.

There are a dozen scenes in all. London, as might be expected, furnishes the majority, and we have delightful views of 'The Belfry of St. Paul's', 'Old Cheapside' and 'Highgate Hill'. Charming and appropriate to the story as these are, they suffer eclipse, however, by 'The Great Big World' – a gigantic globe – which revolves in a stage sky of Oriental Blue, and reveals through the agency of a brilliant lighting scheme the various countries which constitute our sphere.

Laughter is irresistibly won as certain of the scenes progress. In the beautiful 'Banqueting Hall', for instance, we have a pageant in Eastern costume, and the ladies who pass in review, each suiting her deportment to the quarter whence she is suppose to come, include a jaunty princess from Cowcaddens and a dignified relation from Anniesland.

'Dick Whittington' is such an elaborate pantomime that only one performance can be given each evening. To surmount the

**On Friday 14 December, the Glasgow Food Control Committee
distributed specimen ration tickets amongst the local school children
with the request that they should take them home to their parents. The
children in the photo are from Garnetbank Public School.**

difficulty thus created there will be a matinee each afternoon.'

On 17 December, an armistice agreed between Russia and the Central Powers came into effect.

The Daily Record of Monday 24 December carried a story under the
headline CHRISTMAS CHEER which read:

'Money was spent lavishly in Glasgow on Saturday afternoon and
evening. From an early hour onwards, almost without cessation
and, it seemed, in gathering volume, crowds thronged the shops
specialising in gifts intended for the Christmas and New Year
seasons. Tired saleswomen and men were not at all
sorry when at length closing time arrived.

Determined that their token of goodwill to friends at
a distance should not be late in reaching its destination,
large numbers flocked immediately to the counters of
the Post Offices, which presented a remarkable
animated scene during the crush periods.

For the present the Christmas card, whose vogue of
late years was continuously increasing, is suffering
eclipse. Most people feel that the kindly wishes should
assume a more practical form.

Even the most unobservant could not fail to note the

**The death of Colonel
Fred L. Morrison CB,
of Ashcraig, Kelvinside,
Glasgow was
announced towards the
end of December. He
had died in Egypt.**

A queue outside a shop in Glasgow for margarine and butter on the last Saturday of 1917. People were getting ready for the new year festivities.

increased number of men in khaki who promenaded the streets. Leave to spend their Christmas by the old fireside was a privilege greatly relished and if here and there the voluntary ration scale was exceeded by the warm-hearted housewife, anxious to let the visiting lad enjoy substantial fare, and plenty of it, the offence was not very heinous. In anticipation of the arrival of the boys great preparations had been made.

Decorations were the first thought of the housekeeper, seeing that her bi-annual cleaning was over and done with. As a preliminary, it became necessary to secure a liberal supply of flowers available at the season; and in the second place, whatever was omitted, there must be a few sprigs of mistletoe.

Lack of sugar and butter was bemoaned by numerous housewives. Many queer subterfuges were resorted to in the circumstances. With patriotic gallantry, male guests at some houses took tea unsweetened, leaving the available sugar for the use of the ladies and children; and expressed a preference, not always felt, for jellies and syrups in place of butter or margarine.

Christmas music was sung at many of the churches, particularly during the evening service, yesterday, and the sermons in numerous instances related to the season of goodwill.'

Chapter Five

1918 – The Final Blows

At the beginning of January, almost 100 wounded soldiers from various hospitals in Glasgow were entertained by the Glasgow North-Eastern District of the Scottish Legal Life Assurance Society.

Collections taken for the sick and wounded war horses at the Pavilion Theatre in Glasgow in the first week of January raised a total of £85.

Mr George M. Barnes MP, speaking at St Andrew's Hall on the evening of 13 January, said that there had been many strikes since the war began, especially in the recent months, and suggested that the men striking for more pay were no better than profiteers.

He added: 'It is not the poorest amongst us who decide to strike. It is those with relatively high wages. It is those already making £4 or £5 a week who are striking.'

In a reference to housing, Mr Barnes stated that much of the accommodation provided today

An advert in *The Daily Record* of Monday 14 January encouraging people to buy National War Bonds at the Glasgow Tank.

A photo of 'Julian', the Tank-Bank, in place opposite the Glasgow Municipal Buildings on Monday 14 January. Glasgow promised to raise more than the record sum taken by Birmingham which amounted to £6½ million.

was a disgrace for civilization, let alone a Christian community.

In the second week of January, 'Julian', the Tank-Bank, took up quarters opposite the Glasgow Municipal Buildings. Lord Provost J.W. Stewart told the Mayor of Birmingham: 'You can rely upon every man, woman and child on the Clyde to meet Birmingham's challenge.'

The challenge was to beat Birmingham who had previously raised £6½ million through the tank bank.

On Monday 14 January, Glasgow experienced the coldest weather for many years. On Sunday night, 32 degrees of frost were registered in the city. Many householders were without either hot or cold water due to the conditions.

Throughout the day, snow fell persistently throughout Glasgow and the surrounding areas and by evening, it was 4 inches deep. Pedestrians and horses had to take great care. The tramway company brought in their snow plough to keep the route clear.

The cold weather led to many accidents, some fatal. A sledging accident was reported in *The Daily Record* of 14 January:

'When sledging in Thornwood Avenue, Glasgow, on Saturday, three boys knocked down Mrs Maud Williams (32), 10 Hozier Street, Partick. She was picked up semi-conscious and carried to a house where she recovered sufficiently to be able to walk home.

An advert in *The Daily Record* of Tuesday 15 January announcing that the Royal Polytechnic Ltd of Argyle Street would be giving away £500 of War Savings Certificates at the Tank Bank.

People buying War Bonds and War Savings Certificates in the City Chambers on Monday 14 January. By the end of the first day of the Tank Bank, Glasgow had already raised £1 million.

Neil Black Carmichael (14), son of Gilbert Carmichael, 378 Allison Street, Glasgow, while tobogganing in Queen's Park Recreation Ground, sustained a compound fracture of the leg by being thrown out of his sledge, which had collided with a goal post.'

The scene at Glasgow Cross as 'Julian', the tank bank, travelled along Argyle Street and was met by a huge crowd of enthusiastic onlookers.

In January 1918, sugar was rationed. By the end of April, meat, butter, margarine and cheese were also rationed. Ration cards were issued and people were required to register with their local butcher and grocer. People in Glasgow joined long queues to get the basic of foods including potatoes and many other vegetables.

The Daily Record of Saturday 2 February carried the story of a street singer who was due to appear at the Coliseum:

> 'Starring on the programme of the Coliseum next week is Theresa Collins, the little street singer whose history is a romance of natural merit coming to its own.
>
> Miss Collins was discovered singing in Bath Street on Hogmanay, 1917, in a wonderful rich soprano. Though her voice is perfectly natural and untrained, she has no knowledge of music. Recently, she achieved success when singing in St Andrew's Hall at a war-fund concert. Those who heard her then have little doubt that she will be equally successful in her professional career.'

At the beginning of February, while endeavouring to put on the rear-wheel break while driving a horse and lorry, John J. Sweeney, aged 15, of 41 Grove Street, Glasgow, slipped and fell under the wheel which passed over him. He died instantly.

On Saturday 9 February, *The Daily Record* reported that two Russians, Leopold and Louis Coorsh of Hospital Street, Glasgow, together with Harry Levine of Cartside Street, Glasgow, were charged with trying to cross over to Ireland without the permission of the Aliens'

The Anchor liner *Tuscania* was torpedoed on the evening of Tuesday 5 February. On board were 2,011 American troops. The photo shows the wives of the crew waiting outside the Anchor Line Buildings in Glasgow for news.

H. McDonald and A. French, two stewards from the *Tuscania*, who were lucky to survive the attack.

Officer. They were also charged with falsely representing to the customs' officer and ship steward that they were of British nationality.

Harry Collins, a photographer from Dublin, was also charged with aiding and abetting.

All men pleaded guilty. The Fiscal stated that the offences were most serious and said that Collins was most

Captain Peter McLean, the captain of the torpedoed vessel *Tuscania*, survived the attack. He was one of the last people to leave the sinking vessel.

to blame having previously received considerable sums to help the fugitives reach Ireland. The government pressed for a heavy penalty and each man was fined £50 with an alternative of three months in prison.

In *The Daily Record* of 15 February, an article appeared under the headline, 18-YEAR-OLD RECRUITS. It read:

'Men born in 1900 are called upon to report themselves for joining the Colours on the thirtieth day after attaining their eighteenth birthday.

According to the proclamation, a calling-up notice is not necessary and, whether a youth receives a notice or not, he will be regarded as an absentee if he fails to report on the date specified.

Those, of course, who have made application for exemption, and whose cases have not been finally disposed of, are exceptions.'

During February, a whist drive and free gift sale, organised by the employees of Messrs Copland & Lye of Glasgow, raised over £120 in aid of the Royal Infirmary. The employees had also, at other events, raised

On Friday 9 February, there was a meeting of Clyde workers at Messrs Meehan, Scotstoun. The picture shows workers cheering the Government's new Man-Power proposals.

Sergeant John Macaulay VC, (Scots Guards) was home on leave during February and visited his old comrades at the Northern Police Station on Friday 8 February before visiting Plean, his birthplace.

£650 for the war fund and other charities.

At the beginning of March, *The Daily Record* reported the story of a Glasgow airman's death:

'A verdict of accidental death was recorded at an inquest in the Eastern Counties, yesterday, on Second Lieutenant Andrew Ramsay Aitken, of Glasgow, an observer in the Royal Flying Corps. His machine, when landing, collided with a tree, which took off the left wing. When the pilot got out of the machine, he found Aitkin lying unconscious about five yards away.

On 3 March, Russia signed a peace treaty with the Central Powers known as the Treaty of Brest Litovsk.

On Tuesday 5 March, the Prince of Wales visited Glasgow and toured the Clyde shipyards. Whilst in Glasgow, he inspected the officers and men of the merchant service who had been torpedoed. The inspection took place at St Enoch's Station. Altogether, there were 154 officers and men on parade as well as two of the stewardesses who were on board the *Tuscania*, Mrs Carson and Mrs Collins. The prince spoke to a number of the officers and men as well as both ladies before departing to a ringing volley of cheers. Afterwards, he visited the Kenilworth Admiralty Hostel where he was received by Mr Alexander Walker, the district director of labour and housing.

On Wednesday 13 March, Sergeant J. McAulay VC DCM, a former member of the Glasgow police force, was presented with a silver cigar and cigarette casket, together with a silver cigarette case, by his comrades in the Scots Guards. The presentation was made by Major the Earl of Stair, who commanded the reserve battalion of the Scots Guards. Sergeant McAulay was due to attend an investiture at Buckingham Palace the following morning.

In the second week of March, George Henry Hodgetts, a soldier, was sentenced to 12 months' imprisonment at Glasgow Sheriff Court for committing bigamy.

On Saturday 16 March, an Irish Flag Day collection took place in Glasgow. Its aim was to raise funds for the limbless soldiers at Erskine House, the Soldiers' and Sailors' Help Fund, as well as to help the widows, orphans and dependants of the Ancient Order of Hibernians (AOH) who have lost their lives in the Great War.

The Prince of Wales chatting to Ensign Commander Cox on Tuesday 6 March. He was given the heartiest welcome from Clyde workers, several of whom had the honour of meeting him.

The Prince of Wales can be seen using a pneumatic riveting hammer at the yards of Messrs Dunlop while on a visit to Glasgow in the early part of March. 'This thing is jolly heavy,' he said.

On 21 March the Germans launched a massive offensive on the Western Front in a bid to achieve victory before the US forces could be fully deployed.

On Monday 8 April, War Weapons Week began in Scotland. The campaign was launched in Glasgow on Saturday 6 April at an enthusiastic meeting in the Berkeley Hall. Members of war savings committees attended as well as many munition workers. Lord Strathclyde, who chaired the meeting, said: 'The events of the past 14 days have made the pacifist as extinct as the Dodo – they would require to search for the pacifist in the asylums of the country.' This was met with much laughter and applause.

Mr Dalrymple, the manager of the Glasgow tramways, told the meeting that he had a scheme on hand to raise £100,000 for the city's Dreadnought. He suggested that 100,000 citizens join a War Savings Association each contributing £1. A prize scheme was offered by the tramways with 300 prizes totalling, altogether, £7,500. The top prize was £2,500.

The Daily Record reported:

'Each night this week there will be an electric display at the Tramway Offices, Bath Street. All the latest photos from the Front will be shown on a screen.'

A letter appeared in *The Daily Record* of Saturday 13 April under the headline A TOMBOLA GRUMBLE. It read:

'Sir, Some few months ago, Mr Dalrymple, of the Glasgow Corporation Tramways, had in operation a scheme for raising money for various war funds, which, thanks to the effort of a few who have the good name of Glasgow at heart, was forbidden, as it constituted an offence under the Lotteries Act.

He has now a somewhat similar scheme on foot to raise money for Glasgow's Super-Dreadnought. The scheme may escape the fate of the last one but there is no getting away from the fact that it is a lottery. Are we of Glasgow, who enjoy the reputaion of being respectable and law-abiding people, to have that reputation soiled by Mr Dalrymple's schemes?

The cause may be a good one; if so, let us raise money for it by other means.

LEONIDAS.'

Alfred Ash, of the Cameronians, an escaped prisoner of war, took part in the Flag Day celebrations on Saturday 13 April.

It was followed by another letter from a reader signing himself 'BOW-WOW' which read:

'Sir, Do your correspondents who write about the dog nuisance wish to convey the idea that the Almighty made a ridiculous mistake when He created these poor dumb animals, and that He made a worse blunder when He let Noah take two of them into the Ark?

If Noah could tolerate a couple of them within the narrow confines of the Ark, not to mention a whole menagerie of dirtier animals than dogs, surely your correspondents could tolerate dogs that don't belong to them. Perhaps some of them belong to men who are fighting for us?

My brother, who has been in France about two years, owns a dog. His wife and child find the animal a good guard and pet during their loved one's absence. It would be jolly hard if they had to pay £1 tax because grousers like your correspondents hate this specimen of the Creator's handiwork.'

As the collection of funds during War Weapon Week came to an end in April, *The Daily Record* reported on the friendly competition between two cities:

'Rivalry on a friendly nature, but still of the keenest, marks the close of War Weapons Week in Scotland. Edinburgh and Glasgow, who have led throughout the campaign, are at the moment separated by a comparatively small amount.

To the satisfaction of those in the West, the proud position which the East had maintained since the start of the contest was yesterday challenged with success.

Edinburgh yesterday invested £440,596 compared with Glasgow's £757,569. The total obtained by the former is thus brought up to £2,041,079, while the Glasgow figures read £2,065,645.

Arrangements have been made for the head offices of the various banks in Glasgow to remain open until 2 o'clock this afternoon.

Two prize schemes will be in operation in Glasgow today. Particular appeal is made to ladies by the proprietors of the Polytechnic, who have decided to give away twenty-five finely-tailored costumes, each valued at ten guineas.

The other scheme, promoted by the members of the Royal Exchange, has made possible the distribution of £500 among investors. Each purchaser is to receive a voucher on presenting the Certificate or War Bond at the stamping counter.

There is to be a display of manoeuvring by airmen over Glasgow today again.'

In reply to Mr Shinwell at Glasgow Corporation on Thursday 2 May, the town clerk stated that the total number of prosecutions for food adulteration, during the 12 months ending March 1918, amounted to eighty-nine. Of the eighty-eight convictions obtained, seventy-six were for weak milk, three for skimmed and nine for butter.

The first house-to-house collection of scrap metal in Glasgow was carried out on Saturday 4 May as part of a new campaign for the war effort.

General Smuts speaking to Mr Fyfe, the carpenters' foreman at Messrs Henderson's yard at Meadowside, in May.

In the second week in May, Mr P.J. Mackie, in fulfilling an offer he made during Tank Week, placed the sum of £300 at the disposal of the Glasgow War Savings Committee for distribution as prizes.

Every member of the Glasgow War Savings' Association who purchased War Savings Certificates between 1 May and 31 December was entitled to participate in the scheme.

On Saturday 18 May, *The Daily Record* reported that General Smuts had received the freedom of the city of Glasgow:

'General Smuts visited Glasgow yesterday and put in a hard day's work. Between the breakfast hour and half past four in the afternoon, the distinguished soldier and statesman delivered six speeches. In the earlier part of his tour, he addressed workers at Fairfield and Clydebank, and a fact of interest in these assemblies was that numbers who stood around listening, in the days of the South African War, were in the British ranks opposing the then Boer leader.

His most important utterance was reserved for a great meeting at S. Andrew's Hall, at which he discussed, among other topics, three great results that had accrued from the German offensive – unity of command, the awakening of Britain to the peril which threatened, and the arrival of America on the scene of action.

The occasion was an interesting one personally, for at the outset, he was admitted a burgess of the city. Fronting him was a magnificent audience, who filled every part of the large building, and beside him on the platform were Lord Provost Stewart, the Duke of Montrose, Lord Newlands, Lord Inverclyde, Sir Joseph Maclay, Sir John Lindsay and the Magistrates in their ermine.

General Smuts spoke for an hour and five minutes and rose to address the meeting at 3.20. An ovation greeted him. The organ broke into 'He's a Jolly Good Fellow', and the audience, upstanding, joined heartily in the chorus, hats and handkerchiefs being waved as an accompaniment.'

In June, for falsely stating in an application for a sugar card for herself and her family, that no other application was made, Elizabeth Keatings was fined £1 at Glasgow Sheriff Court.

Police issued a warning to the people of Glasgow in June to look out for forged £1 treasury notes. They stated that the notes in their possession were of poor quality with faulty colouring and drawing.

A letter appeared in *the Daily Record* on Wednesday 19 June from a soldier's wife. It read:

'Sir, I think it is high time that something was done to increase dependants' allowances. They are not getting enough to keep body and soul together. I myself am a soldier's wife with four children, and I find it impossible to pay rent, clothes, insurance, food and light off my weekly allowance of 31s – an average of 6s 2½d a head. They talk about increasing the population. The more kiddies there are the less we get. It is a crying shame that we should have to depend on our husbands to send us a few shillings saved out of their bob a day to get the kiddies clothes.'

Red Cross Week was held in Glasgow in the second part of June to raise funds for wounded soldiers. Events included fetes, sales and sports gatherings.

As part of Red Cross Week, a naval ambulance train was on exhibition at the Central Station, Glasgow. Admission to see the train was one shilling and every two-hundredth person received a War Savings Certificate. On the first day, the train attracted 2,000 sightseers and raised funds of £102.

A raid at a pawnshop in Glasgow was reported in *The Daily Record* of Friday 21 June:

'Particulars of an amusing exploit in a pawnshop were related in Glasgow Sheriff Court yesterday when John Porteous was sent to prison for four months for assaulting and attempting to rob one of the women assistants.

Porteous went into the shop and bought a South African War medal. On being shown a brooch, he threw an overcoat over the shop assistant's head, dragged her into the back shop, knocked her down, and demanded back the money he paid for the medal. He managed to escape at the time but was arrested later.

It was stated that Porteous had joined the Army three times and had been as often discharged after being confined in asylums. He said he had no recollection of the affair.

The Fiscal said Porteous had been under observation but could not be certified insane.'

The Daily Record of Friday 28 June reported on a missing soldier:

'Mr and Mrs Massie, 12 Prince Albert Street, Strathbungo, Glasgow, have received word from their son, Private M. Massie, Black Watch, that he is a prisoner in Germany and unwounded. Private Massie was reported missing in the big offensive last March.'

At the beginning of July, John Blair, a foreman labourer, and Thomas Doran, also a labourer, both from Glasgow, were sentenced to 14 days imprisonment, with hard labour, for having been drunk while working in a shell-filling factory. Sheriff Blair commented on their stupidity and pointed out that they didn't seem to realize the danger that they were putting their fellow workers in.

The Glasgow Fair holiday began on Thursday 11 July with shipbuilders, engineering and other public works closing down for ten days. For the few days previous and especially on 10 July, large crowds of holiday seekers left the city and headed for the coast and countryside. An exceptionally large demand was made on the Irish steamers and by Tuesday, every available foot of room aboard the ferry to Belfast had been taken.

Thomas Whalon, a Glasgow excursionist, had an unfortunate experience at Greenock. While walking onto a steamer, he overbalanced and fell into the water. By the time he was rescued, he was exhausted and a doctor recommended that he be taken to the infirmary.

On 15 July, the Second Battle of the Marne began. Tens of thousands of men were killed but the counter-attack at the Marne was one of the first series of offensives by the Allies which would ultimately lead to the end of the war.

The Daily Record of Thursday 25 July reported on the grip of influenza in larger Scottish towns. The story read:

'According to a report issued by the Registrar General, the deaths from influenza for the week ending July 20 in the principal towns of Scotland numbered 19; while in 79 deaths classified as due to other diseases, influenza was a contributory cause.

In the previous weeks, the deaths numbered 26 and 74 respectively.

Influenza has attacked many people in Greenock and ten deaths from the disease were registered last week. Nine of the fatal cases were adults. As a precautionary measure, the infirmary has been closed to visitors.'

The flu epidemic of 1918 would later spread worldwide and kill more people than the Great War itself.

In July it was announced that 2,000 women were employed on the tramcars in Glasgow. Of those, 423 acted as drivers, the most female drivers in any part of the United Kingdom.

Towards the end of July a complaint by farmers was raised in Glasgow and the story was carried in the newspapers of the day:

'Presiding over the summer conference of the Scottish Chamber of Agriculture in Glasgow, Mr Hugh W.B. Crawford stated that in the South of Scotland, with the announcement that no soldiers were to be given to help with the harvest, the situation was very serious indeed. They were perfectly ashamed that the Government had not kept faith with the farmers in this matter. Everything must bow to the winning of the war, but when the Government call up men they ought to provide for labour to take their places.'

On Monday 5 August, the send-off of the tank bank at Greenock was reported:

'Speaking from the top of the tank, "Julian", at Greenock on Saturday, Lord Strathclyde said that he did not believe in negotiations for peace. The great death struggle which we were fighting now was not going to be decided by negotiations. It was for everyone to invest in the national concern and they would have the British Empire behind them for security.

In his opinion, the War Savings movement would become a permanent method by which money would be raised to run our own country.

In less than an hour, a sum of £100,000 was subscribed and during the evening, there was a fairly brisk demand at the Post Office for War Certificates.

"Julian" remains at Cathcart Square until tonight.'

Violet Watson, who lived in Parkhead, Glasgow and was employed at a munitions factory, was fined £3 in August, with the option of 20 day in prison, for stealing a silk scarf from another worker in the shifting house. *The Daily Record* of Thursday 22 August carried a story under the headline DOG ON GUARD DUTY. It read:

'Mrs Bowder, 3 Shaftesbury Terrace, Glasgow, owner of Barrie, the St Bernard lent to the War Office, has been informed that the dog passed every test splendidly, and within a week of his arrival at the war dogs' school was sent out on active service. Major Richardson is proud of his Glasgow recruit and advises Mrs Bowder that Barrie is now doing his duty on guard work with the army somewhere in France.'

Towards the end of August, the sum of £645 was handed over to the treasurer of the Police Prisoners of War Fund. The money was raised at the Glasgow police sports day at Ibrox Park.

A Russian, who failed to notify his change of residence in Glasgow, was fined £2 in August with the alternative of ten days' imprisonment. He was discovered at his new lodgings hiding under the bed.

On 29 August, an unusual theft in Glasgow was reported:

'On a charge of breaking into a bonded store in Glasgow and stealing several bottles of whisky, two soldiers and two civilians have been remitted to the Sheriff from Glasgow St Rollox Police Court. It is alleged that the puttees of the soldiers were tied together and the smallest and lightest of the men was lowered into the store from a skylight window of the saloon. By the improvised rope, the bottles, which were put in a couple of bags, were hoisted to the skylight.'

At the beginning of September, twenty members of the Glasgow police force travelled to assist the harvesting operations in Lanarkshire and Dumfriesshire. Many more were sent to other districts in the following days.

On Monday 16 September, Jacob Gabrilovitz, a Jewish butcher, was fined £50 at Glasgow Sheriff Court for sending a false return to the local food committee. He stated that 1,176 adults and 324 children had registered with him using their rationing cards. The truth was that only 816 adults and 178 children had registered.

James Grant, a provision merchant, of 773 New City Road, Glasgow was fined £5 for selling ½lb of uncooked ham and ½lb of margarine to a person who wasn't a registered customer.

Annie Tyrrel was sent to jail for 21 days in September for pickpocketing from ladies in the General Post Office in Glasgow. She was also charged with stealing 26s and 2d and a first class season ticket.

During September, Sheriff Craigie of Glasgow, fined the wife of a soldier 5s for sending matches in the post. When the package was stamped, the matches ignited. Sheriff Craigie warned that a higher penalty would be imposed in future similar cases.

The Daily Record of Thursday 19 September reported on a case which had come before the courts:

> 'A fine of a guinea, with the option of 14 days in prison, was imposed at Maryhill Police Court, Glasgow, on an elderly woman, Mary Bell, who was convicted of having stolen three turnips from a field at Kelvinside. She was seen by a policeman to pull the turnips and wrap them in her shawl.'

Meanwhile, a seven year old boy, Archibald Duffy Mellison, of 12 Anderson Street, Kinning Park, Glasgow, died while hanging onto the rear end of a lorry, loaded with heavy machinery cases when one of the cases fell on him.

At the end of September, two youths who were seen loitering suspiciously at the corner of Duke Street and Bluevale Street, Glasgow, were arrested and in their possession were found burglars' tools. At the Eastern Police Court, the elder boy, William Thomson, was sent to prison for 60 days while the younger boy, James Bell, received 12 strokes of the birch.

A new boat train was announced in *The Daily Record* of Monday 30 September:

> 'In the interest of all ranks on leave from the Expeditionary Forces it has been arranged that a train will, on and after October 1, leave Glasgow Central Station daily (Sundays included) at 8.45 p.m., and arrive in London (Euston Station) at 6.30 a.m.
>
> This will enable soldiers to make the necessary connection for the leave train from Victoria Station, London, to both Folkestone and Dover.
>
> Hitherto, officers and men who have had to return from Glasgow and neighbourhood by the 4.35 p.m. train from Glasgow Central will, under the new regime, be able to spend an additional afternoon at home.
>
> All Naval and Military passengers must, however, bear in mind that the 9.45 p.m. ex Central – Naval and Military portion – will be withdrawn on 1st October, and that the last train for London leaves Glasgow Central Station at 8.45 p.m.'

On Tuesday 1 October, the Glasgow and South Western Railway brought into effect a restricted train service due to the shortage of coal. The restrictions were set to last as coal was vitally needed to transport food traffic and munitions of war. It was asked that the public refrain from train travel unless absolutely necessary.

Glasgow Flag Day fell on 5 October and supported the Harry Lauder £1,000,000 fund for Scottish sailors and soldiers.

During October, it was reported that £220 had been collected since the previous November by the workers of Mile End, Glasgow who organised concerts every Friday afternoon. The money went towards a fund used to purchase articles or comforts for wounded soldiers in Oakland and Maryhill Barracks hospitals.

On Thursday 24 October, forty-four apprentices were charged, at a special sitting of the Glasgow Munition Tribunal, with absenting themselves from their work without leave. Five, who had previously been warned, were fined 15s while the others were fined 10s. Three men who were charged with playing cards during the nightshift were each fined £3.

On 9 November, Kaiser Wilhelm II abdicated and fled Germany.

When the Armistice was agreed between the Allies and the Germans, the fighting in Europe came to an end. It went into effect at 11am on 11 November. When the news reached Britain, people throughout the land took to the streets to celebrate.

The Daily Record of Tuesday 12 November carried the news of the Armistice celebrations in Glasgow:

'The people of Glasgow, who had exercised commendable restraint since the rumour of an armistice, let themselves go to an amazing extent yesterday morning when the glad news told that the Great War was at an end.

The news was broadcast early in a special edition of the "Noon Daily Record", copies of which were eagerly purchased and the heart-stirring news spread like wildfire from the centre to circumference of the city.

In a surprisingly short time, flags were being flown over all the major buildings including the General Post Office.

Lines of streamers were rigged from one side of the street to the other in some of the principal thoroughfares and elaborate preparations were afoot to decorate more lavishly the streets and other prominent buildings with trophies and an array of flags. The Merchants' House in George Square at first showed only the Stars and Stripes but very speedily the Union Jack flew as well in the breeze.

Meantime, a wonderful transformation occurred in the streets converging at the Municipal Buildings. People ran or marched in groups towards George Square and quickly a dense crowd had amassed, filling the space right from the City Chambers and over into George Square. The area was crowded with a seething mass, animated with enthusiasm. Songs and choruses were sung. Flags of all sizes were produced and fluttered above the heads of the people producing kaleidoscope effects.

Every class of citizen was represented in the cheering throng. Great companies of warehouse girls, who by consent had left work; munition girls still wearing their overalls; male munition workers also in their working attire, in many cases having travelled in hired motor lorries: and groups of American and Overseas troops in khaki, with flags on their picturesque hats, formed the larger proportion of the gathering but there was also a very considerable sprinkling of city clerks and other workmen.

Happiness beamed on every countenance with endless hand-shaking and congratulations. "Thank God it is all over" was the fervently-expressed sentiment to be heard on every hand.

Many adventurous youths climbed up on the pedestals of the statues in the Square, and still more enterprising, youths of both sexes mounted on the ledges of the facade on either side of the loggia of the City Chambers. Among these were wounded soldiers from the hospitals. Some of these who had use of their legs danced on elevated positions in the madness and joy, to the intense delight of onlookers.

Making a way through the jubilant crowd, one could not but be thrilled by the constant incidents obtruding themselves, all of them illustrating the depth of the feelings which the young and old expressed.

There were large cries for the Lord Provost, and his Lordship, on his way to a meeting of the Clyde Trust, essayed to address the assembled multitude in front of the City Chambers.

It was from a lorry he made the attempt, but it was only an attempt, because the jubilation of the crowd was so ear-filling that it was not possible for any man without a megaphone to make himself heard. To make matters worse, the horse yoked to the lorry, seemed to be of pro-German tendency, for he did not help the situation, by cavorting about and even standing on his hind legs.

The crowd at Buckingham Palace on Armistice Day. Thousands of cheering spectators lined the streets to celebrate the end of the war.

However, his Lordship was understood to say that he spoke for the whole of the citizens of Glasgow when he congratulated all upon the glorious victories of the Allies and the end of the Great War.

His Lordship authorised the breaking out of flags on all public buildings and at the public parks.

In the outskirts, as in the heart of the city, the news ran like a flame. Bunting at once became a necessity of first importance; and soon from window and doorway fluttered gaily the emblems of rejoicing. Every shop which sold flags of any texture or size was besieged. No one grudged the figure demanded for the possession of the coveted trophies. The poorest appeared to think a flag at 5s was dirt cheap; and one large firm estimated that in the course of an hour, they disposed of £2,000 worth of bunting.

Small parties from every point of the compass sought the main arteries of the city to demonstrate by flag, voice and musical instrument their heartfelt delight at the cessation of fighting.

Colonial soldiers, encountered by the way, were the subject of enviable attention on the part of merry munitionettes. And the soldiers, brave boys, did not flinch from the ordeal, although on occasions the amiability of their fair admirers attracted a good deal of amused notice.

Sights calculated to touch tender chords were also in evidence. One was witnessed in Jamaica Street. Lying at full length in a bath chair was a poor wounded boy. In his right hand was the Union Jack, the flag he had defended to his bodily cost, and on his face was a smile of unaffected pleasure as he waved the red, white and blue. Behind him, and acting as his coachmen, came a couple of stout comrades, also in the uniform of convalescence. Way for the trio was made by everyone as the triumphal car, for it seemed no less, passed down towards the bridge.

Sailormen from ships in the harbour had also come to town. Both services mingled on occasions. From out of the way corners, they had secured musical instruments of weird design and expression. Playing these, they marched through the streets, a source of amusement alike to themselves and to the thousands who lined the footways.

The sense of humour, which has been the salvation of "Tommy" throughout the fighting, did not desert him in the hour of victory.

Armistice celebrations with many happy faces and much flag waving. American flags were waved alongside British ones and everyone was jubilant that the war was finally over.

> Seeing on a notice board at Central Station the words, "Soldiers returning to France", a joyful party promptly erased the words, to emphasise their mission across the Channel was now happily at an end.'

The first batch of Scottish prisoners from Germany, after the Armistice was signed, arrived back in Scotland on Wednesday 20 November. Among them were several men belonging to naval units who, after the fall of Antwerp, had escaped to Holland where they had been interned for the past four years.

The war had been a long and bloody one. Glasgow had played a major part in the struggle. With the war over, there wasn't a family in Glasgow who hadn't lost a husband, son, father, nephew, uncle or brother. There were tremendous celebrations in the streets as the end of the war was announced but the effects of the conflict lasted for years to come.

Acknowledgements

Thanks to the helpful and friendly team at Pen and Sword including Roni Wilkinson, Matt Jones, Jon Wilkinson, Irene Moore, Diane Parkin, Katie Eaton, Laura Lawton and Jodie Butterwood.

Thanks also to Tina Cole and Tilly Barker.

Sources:
The Aberdeen Evening Express
The Daily Mirror
The Daily Record
The Dundee Courier
The Dundee Evening Telegraph
The Edinburgh Evening News
The Evening Dispatch
The Evening Herald
The Falkirk Herald
The Hamilton Advertiser
The Manchester Courier and Lancashire General Advertiser
The West Briton and Cornwall Advertiser
The Yellowstone News

Index